The Heritage of Literature Series

The Royal Hunt of the Sun

D1151869

The Heritage of Literature Series

This series incorporates titles under the following headings: Travel and Adventure, Animal Stories, Fiction, Modern Classics, Short Stories, Prose Writing, Drama, Myths and Legends, Poetry.

Other titles in the Modern Classics Section of the series include:

ANIMAL FARM *George Orwell*
VOSS *Patrick White*
SCOOP *Evelyn Waugh*
THE GOSHAWK *T. H. White*
UNDER THE NET *Iris Murdoch*
THE WESKER TRILOGY *Arnold Wesker*
EXCEPT THE LORD *Joyce Cary*
GO TELL IT ON THE MOUNTAIN *James Baldwin*
THE WAY OF ALL FLESH *Samuel Butler*
CRY, THE BELOVED COUNTRY *Alan Paton*
THE LONELINESS OF THE LONG-DISTANCE RUNNER, *Alan Sillitoe and Billy Liar*
KEITH WATERHOUSE (in one volume)

A complete list of the series is available on request.

The Royal Hunt of the Sun

A Play Concerning the Conquest of Peru

by

PETER SHAFFER

With Introduction by

A. W. ENGLAND

and Historical Note, Notes and Exercises by

JOHN W. MACDONALD and JOHN C. SAXTON

LONGMAN

LONGMAN GROUP LIMITED
London

*Associated companies, branches and representatives
throughout the world*

This edition © Longman Group Ltd (formerly
Longmans, Green & Co Ltd) 1966

*This edition first published by Longman Group Ltd
(formerly Longmans, Green & Co Ltd) in association
with Messrs Hamish Hamilton Ltd 1966
Fifth impression 1974*

ISBN 0 582 34892 7

*The cover photograph of Robert Stephens as Atahuallpa in
the National Theatre production is by Angus McBean.*

*Printed in Hong Kong by
Dai Nippon Printing Co (H.K.) Ltd*

CONTENTS

NORTH AMERICA

ATLANTIC OCEAN

St. Augustini 1565

Havana 1515

Mexico 1521

Panama 1519

Tumbez
Cajamarca
Lima 1535

R. AMAZON

Equator

SOUTH AMERICA

oCuzco – Pizarro came here 1532

R. PARANÁ

PACIFIC OCEAN

Santiago 1541

RIO DE LA PLATA

Occupied by Spanish

- - - - 1492–1543
- - - - 1543–1600

0 200   1000

Miles at the Equator

HISTORICAL NOTE

Spain's Golden Age of Expansion

In medieval Europe one of the major sources of wealth was spices, which for centuries had made their tortuous way from the East Indies to the Mediterranean by what came to be known as 'the overland route'. The cities of northern Italy which were the gateways to Europe in monopolizing this trade had amassed considerable fortunes in the process.

With the rise of Europe's nation-states in the fifteenth and sixteenth centuries, particularly in Spain and Portugal, this monopoly was seriously challenged for the first time. In the quest for an alternative sea route the Portuguese ventured south around Africa to India and the spice islands beyond. The Spaniards on the other hand sailed west, and with Columbus's discovery of the Bahamas in 1492 a new exciting chapter in Western history opened. While these islands were unimportant in themselves since they were not the fabled Indies, it did mean that Spanish eyes were turned permanently westward to what soon came to be realized as a vast, unknown continent.

With the discovery of America, Spain's maritime policy began to alter its purpose. The interest in spices was replaced by a new greed when rare metals and precious stones were discovered. The original dream of spices began to fade as the early explorers plucked silver and gold from the natives and sent them home to a delighted monarch.

The rich fertility of the new lands was another attraction, a striking contrast to the arid soil of Spain. Families were transported westward in the reasonable expectation of a more prosperous living, so that the new virgin territory began to be permanently settled in a very short time.

There was another incentive – the challenge that lay in the conversion of the heathen Indians. While of prime concern to the papacy, it was also important enough to Charles V, King of Spain and Holy Roman Emperor, to figure very large in his plans, a design for power which would extend both his empire and the Catholic faith at the same time. For the Church it was obviously important to convert the heathen, since it gave the Pope an opportunity to shore up his realm, shaken by losses to the Protestant faiths in Europe. New Spain thus offered a fresh field in the winning of new souls to a Church seriously depleted. Since in the Church's eyes the heathen were as much the Anti-Christ as the Protestants of Europe, any means of persuasion was justified, even the most brutal, as long as their conversion could be realized. Because salvation could be expected only inside the Faith, any method to secure conversion was sanctioned. This practice of forced conversion does, of course, play a very large part in the story of this drama, particularly in the conversion of Atahuallpa.

So powerful were the economic and religious motives that drove Spain in its course of discovery and colonization, that within fifty years of Columbus's voyage its representatives had won control of the entire Caribbean and Central America. They had also conquered, in the process, the two greatest civilizations of the New World, the Aztecs in Mexico and the Incas in Peru.

This achievement would have been impossible without the right men, and Spain had them in a body that came to be known as the *conquistadores* (the conquerors). Popular legend often paints these men in romantic hues, but more often than not they were from the dregs of society. Spain was still a completely feudal society: in it were two basic classes – those with land, and (the majority) those without. It was very nearly impossible for a landless opportunist to better himself. Unlike England, Spain had no real trading tradition nor commercial middle class, so that the only way the landless peasants or the lower nobility could escape its grinding poverty was to ship out to the uncertain glories of the beckoning West. The stubborn determination of Pizarro and his men should not thus surprise us. The cruel suffering and misfortunes which they bore were quite simply born of desperation. In the Americas there was excitement and the lure of fortune, for which the *conquistadores* were willing to gamble with their very lives.

Historical Note

The Kingdom of the Incas

In 1492, Peru, although unknown to the West, was already an empire three centuries old. Isolated from the rest of South America by the Andes and the Amazon jungle, its inhabitants had developed sophisticated agricultural methods to wring subsistence from a dry and hostile soil.

In the centuries after A.D. 1200 the Incas, by lengthy conquest, extended their hegemony to an area of 350,000 square miles occupying all of Peru and extending into Ecuador in the north and Chile in the south. Although several thousand miles long, the kingdom was never more than two hundred miles wide; so, in order to survive, the rulers developed a strongly centralized form of government with its capital at Cuzco. This strong centralization was reason for both its amazing efficiency and its equally amazing sudden and total collapse.

In the state, the most important economic group was the *ayllu* or clan. It corresponded to a community occupying a certain area in which all arable land was divided into three parts. The largest section was for the people's use with enough soil to support all those who had to live off it. When each male member of the community set up a home after marriage at twenty-five, he became known as a *puric* and was given enough land to maintain himself and family. After the people's basic needs had been satisfied, the rest of the land in the *ayllu* was divided between the Church and the State. Every *puric* was required periodically to work on this land as a form of taxes. The produce of the State lands fed the army and the small number of executive officials (usually related to the Inca) and the surplus was stored in large warehouses throughout the land. When a particular *ayllu* suffered disaster or a crop failure these stored foodstuffs were doled out during the emergency. Consequently there was no need for currency, and none was used. Goods were exchanged at local fairs by means of barter.

Within each *ayllu* and over the entire state every child and adult had his appointed task. Boys from nine to sixteen, for

ix

example, were expected to act as shepherds to the state llama herds, while men over sixty acted as schoolteachers or tended the community's poultry. Each male *puric*, in addition to working on the state lands, was required to serve in the army, and in his absence his fields were cultivated by the rest of the *ayllu*.

The main problem in such a scattered empire, an empire consisting of (like Russia today) many different tribes, was communication. Like the Romans, the Incas met this difficulty by the construction of a vast system of roads running the length of the 'nation'. At every 'mile' post, relay stages were built with post runners or *chasqui* stationed in each who were required to run to the next post. The roads were invaluable for the expediting of transported goods and messages, as well as for the provision of means of rapid transport for the army to quell any sudden uprising.

All roads led to Cuzco, the fabled capital of Peru where all reports were received by the Sapa Inca. From him all directives issued, and without his command nothing could be undertaken. Venerated as a god, an incarnation of the sun, he ran his empire smoothly with the assistance of an army of retainers but a surprisingly small coterie of officials. The state was an unusual blend of 'socialism' and centralized theocracy.

One very surprising fact about this sophisticated and highly efficient society was the fact that it developed no written languages. All relayed messages were either verbal or in the form of a *quipu*. This was a single thick cord with knots from each of which other cords were strung with their own series of knots. A *quipu* reader, by examining the number and colour of the knots could thereby interpret a fairly lengthy factual message. At best it was a ponderous system.

Peru under the Incas was a quietly contented state without poverty or begging. Artistic expression, particularly in metal craft, reached a high level. Invasion from without was unknown and the rule of the Sapa Inca was in most instances benign. Yet it possessed two great weaknesses which, with the arrival of Pizarro, proved its undoing. The absence of a written language made the communication of a potential threat impossible, since the *quipu* dealt in facts, not ideas or emotions. Secondly, so centralized was the empire that without the Sapa Inca's explicit orders no action could be taken. After Atahuallpa was seized by Pizarro his subjects stood helplessly by because they had never been trained or exposed to the exercise of initiative.

Pizarro and Peru

It is probable that Francisco Pizarro was born in 1471. What is certain is that he was illegitimate, that he grew up in the most squalid of rural surroundings, and that he was first heard of as a soldier in Hispaniola in 1510. A year later he was a member of Balboa's party which discovered the Pacific. It may have been at this point that Pizarro first heard of the existence of Peru, for tradition suggests that some captive Indians informed Balboa of a great kingdom to the south. Balboa did himself make one fruitless voyage in that direction. Spain's absorption, however, lay in the isthmus territory where a passage through to the Pacific might still be found. The story of Inca gold was discounted as another of the numerous vague rumours with which New Spain abounded.

The Initial Voyages

The rumour, however, was not lost on Pizarro. In 1524 he combined with Diego de Almagro, a middle-aged soldier-of-fortune, and Hernando de Lugue, the Vicar of Panama, both of whom shared his faith and vision. Together they raised enough money to equip a ship and assemble a crew. With the local governor's permission Pizarro set sail from Panama and steered south into unexplored waters. This first voyage proved a nightmare but, despite the terribly heavy seas, Pizarro beat his way further south along the Pacific coast than anyone before him. They did obtain some crude gold ornaments from the few natives they captured but, more important, Pizarro received confirmation of the existence of a great empire further south, an empire rich beyond imagining with gold.

Little notice was taken of Pizarro or his news on his return to Panama, because of the electrifying excitement of Cortes's capture of the Mexican kingdom. The Aztec empire was being methodically plundered by Cortes and his men, so Pizarro's poorly substantiated rumours claimed little attention. Nevertheless a second voyage was fitted out and two ships sailed in 1526 to find the Inca kingdom. After endless difficulties the two ships put back to Panama, leaving Pizarro and sixteen volunteers behind on a small island off the coast of Ecuador. When the relief ship returned nine months later Pizarro persuaded it to continue the search, and sailing south across the equator it put in at Tumbez, a prosperous port in northern Peru. Here they were warmly greeted by the inhabitants and welcomed by an Inca noble of high rank. Here, also, Pizarro enlisted the services of Felipillo, who was to become the party's official interpreter. At last Pizarro's quest was successful, for it established beyond all doubt the existence of a vast empire of high civilization and great wealth.

Upon his return to Panama plans were immediately agreed upon to enlist the approval and support of the royal court of Charles V. Pizarro made his trip back to Spain in 1528 and though King Charles never fully grasped the significance of his report, permission was hesitantly granted for a third voyage. The King also took the precaution of appointing a royal overseer, Miguel Estete, to ensure that the Crown should receive its one-fifth of all the treasure obtained. The King refused to provide Pizarro with any financial assistance. In all history there can be no more marked example of such a niggardly investment reaping so golden a reward.

When Pizarro landed in 1531 at Tumbez for the second time, he was immediately encouraged by the news of fierce civil war within the Inca empire. With the death of the Sapa Inca, Huayana Capac, in 1523, there had broken out a violent and unprecedented conflict over the succession. Two brothers were at odds – Huasar, the legitimate heir, and Atahuallpa, the illegitimate but favoured son. The civil war, which had been a terribly bloody affair, finally terminated in victory for Atahuallpa with a monumental battle in the northern Andes. For this reason, the Inca was not at Cuzco, a thousand miles to the south of Tumbez, but, rather, at Cajamarca, only three hundred and fifty miles away in the mountains. Pizarro could not have been more fortunate; the state was still a disturbed shambles, and the Sapa Inca lay just within reach. It was as though the Fates were atoning for sixty years of miserly encouragement. Already a plan had taken shape in Pizarro's mind and it seems likely that his conversations with Cortes at the Spanish Court had a marked influence on his design. Cortes had seized Montezuma, the Aztec chief, by treachery, and, as a result, had inherited an empire. The lesson was not to be lost on Pizarro, as the story of the play, which begins at this point in history, makes clearly evident.

The Aftermath of the Story

The aftermath of this tale of cupidity and betrayal continues the thread of treachery. Systematically the Spaniards set out to strip the nation of its wealth. Temples were looted, towns were gutted, insurrection sprang up only to be ruthlessly suppressed, and famine and disease were the common lot of the natives. Inevitably the thieves fell out and split into two warring factions, those supporting Pizarro, and those his erstwhile colleague Almagro. Despite the intervention of Charles V, which effected a brief peace, strife broke out again very shortly. It is probably fitting that both disputants should suffer sudden and violent deaths during the course of their struggle. There remains one final irony to the Pizarro story. The gold which had flooded Spain with such an abundance of wealth was responsible for her eventual ruin. With this surfeit of gold, prices rose, inflation was given its head, and Spain started on the steady economic decline from which she has never recovered.

John W. MacDonald
John C. Saxton

The Royal Hunt of the Sun

For

Alan and Paula

with love

AUTHOR'S NOTES

THE TEXT

Each Act contains twelve sections, marked by roman numerals. These are solely for reference, and do not indicate pauses or breaks of any kind. The action is continuous.

THE SET

In this version of the play I refer throughout to the set used by the National Theatre Company at the Chichester Festival 1964. Essentially, all that is required for a production of *The Royal Hunt of the Sun* is a bare stage and an upper level. However, the setting by Michael Annals was so superb, and so brilliantly succeeded in solving the visual problems of the play, that I wish to recall it here in print.

Basically this design consisted of a huge aluminium ring, twelve feet in diameter, hung in the centre of a plain wooden back-wall. Around its circumference were hinged twelve petals. When closed, these interlocked to form a great medallion on which was incised the emblem of the Conquistadors; when opened, they formed the rays of a giant golden sun, emblem of the Incas. Each petal had an inlay of gold magnetized to it: when these inlays were pulled out (in Act II, Scene vi) the great black frame remaining symbolized magnificently the desecration of Peru. The centre of this sun formed an acting area above the stage, which was used in Act I to show Atahuallpa in majesty, and in Act II served for his prison and subsequently for the treasure chamber.

This simple but amazing set was for me totally satisfying on all levels: scenically, aesthetically, and symbolically.

THE MUSIC

The musical excerpts at the end of the book represent the three most easily detached pieces from the remarkable score

B   xvii

composed for the play by Marc Wilkinson. This extraordinary music I believe to be an integral part of any production of *The Royal Hunt of the Sun*. It embraces bird cries; plain-chant; a fantasia for organ; freezing sounds for the Mime of the Great Ascent, and frightening ones for the Mime of the Great Massacre. To me its most memorable items are the exquisitely doleful lament which opens Act II, and, most amazing of all, the final Chant of Resurrection, to be whined and whispered, howled and hooted, over Atahuallpa's body in the darkness, before the last sunrise of the Inca Empire.

The full score can be obtained from the London Authors, 8 Upper Brook Street, London W.1.

THE PRODUCTION

There are, no doubt, many ways of producing this play, as there are of setting it. My hope was always to realise on stage a kind of 'total' theatre, involving not only words but rites, mimes, masks and magics. The text cries for illustration. It is a director's piece, a pantomimist's piece, a musician's piece, a designer's piece, and of course an actor's piece, almost as much as it is an author's. In this edition, as with the set, I have included as many details of the Chichester production as possible, partly because I was deeply involved in its creation, but mainly as a tribute to the superb achievement of John Dexter.

P.S.

Characters of the Play

THE SPANIARDS

The Officers
FRANCISCO PIZARRO, *Commander of the Expedition*
HERNANDO DE SOTO, *Second-in-Command*
MIGUEL ESTETE, *Royal Veedor, or Overseer*
PEDRO DE CANDIA, *Commander of Artillery*
DIEGO DE TRUJILLO, *Master of Horse*

The Men
MARTIN RUIZ
YOUNG MARTIN, *Pizarro's Page: Old Martin as a boy*
SALINAS, *Blacksmith*
RODAS, *Tailor*
VASCA
DOMINGO
JUAN CHAVEZ
PEDRO CHAVEZ

The Priests
FRAY VINCENTE DE VALVERDE, *Chaplain to the Expedition (Dominican)*
FRAY MARCOS DE NIZZA, *Franciscan Friar*

THE INDIANS

ATAHUALLPA, *Sovereign Inca of Peru*
VILLAC UMU, *High Priest of Peru*
CHALLCUCHIMA, *An Inca General*
A CHIEFTAIN
A HEADMAN OF A THOUSAND FAMILIES
FELIPILLO, *An Indian boy, employed by Pizarro as Interpreter*
MANCO, *A Chasqui, or Messenger* (non-speaking)
INTI COUSSI, *Step-sister of Atahuallpa* (non-speaking)
OELLO, *A wife of Atahuallpa* (non-speaking)
SPANISH SOLDIERS AND PERUVIAN INDIANS

xix

Place

Apart from two early scenes in Spain and Panama, the play is set in the Upper Province of the Inca Empire: what is now South Ecuador and North Western Peru. The whole of Act II takes place in the town of Cajamarca.

Time

June 1529 – August 1533

Act I

The Hunt

Act II

The Kill

The Royal Hunt of the Sun was first presented by the National Theatre at Chichester on 7 July 1964 with the following cast:

MARTIN RUIZ	*Robert Lang*
MARTIN RUIZ as a Boy	*Roy Holder*
FRANCISCO PIZARRO	*Colin Blakely*
DIEGO DE TRUJILLO	*Mike Gambon*
SALINAS	*Dan Meaden*
RODAS	*Rod Beacham*
FRAY VINCENTE DE VALVERDE	*Peter Cellier*
VASCA	*Robert Russell*
DOMINGO	*Lewis Fiander*
JUAN CHAVEZ	*Christopher Timothy*
PEDRO CHAVEZ	*Gerald McNally*
HERNANDO DE SOTO	*Michael Turner*
FELIPILLO	*Derek Jacobi*
FRAY MARCOS DE NIZZA	*Edward Caddick*
MIGUEL ESTETE	*James Mellor*
MANCO	*Neil Fitzpatrick*
ATAHUALLPA	*Robert Stephens*
VILLAC UMU	*Edward Petherbridge*
CHALLCUCHIMA	*Edward Hardwicke*
PEDRO DE CANDIA	*Frank Wylie*
CHIEFTAIN	*Peter John*
HEADMAN	*Bruce Purchase*
INTI COUSSI	*Louise Purnell*
OELLO	*Jeanette Landis*

PERUVIAN INDIANS *Michael Byrne, Christopher Chittell, Kurt Christian, Anton Darby, Nicholas Edmett, William Hobbs, Alan Ridgway, John Rogers, Clive Rust*

Production by John Dexter, Desmond O'Donovan
Scenery and Costumes by Michael Annals
Music by Marc Wilkinson
Movement by Claude Chagrin
Lighting by John Read

Act One

A bare stage. On the back wall, which is of wood, hangs a huge metal medallion, quartered by four black crucifixes, sharpened to resemble swords.

I

Darkness.

OLD MARTIN, *grizzled, in his middle fifties, appears. He wears the black costume of a Spanish hidalgo in the mid-sixteenth century.*

OLD MARTIN. Save you all. My name is Martin. I'm a soldier of Spain and that's it. Most of my life I've spent fighting for land, treasure and the cross. I'm worth millions. Soon I'll be dead and they'll bury me out here in Peru, the land I helped ruin as a boy. This story is about ruin. Ruin and gold. More gold than any of you will ever see even if you worked in a counting house. I'm going to tell you how one hundred and sixty-seven men conquered an empire of twenty-four million. And then things that no one has ever told: things to make you groan and cry out I'm lying. And perhaps I am. The air of Peru is cold and sour like in a vault, and wits turn easier here even than in Europe. But grant me this: I saw him closer than anyone, and had cause only to love him. He was my altar, my bright image of salvation. Francisco Pizarro! Time was when I'd have died for him, or for any worship.

YOUNG MARTIN *enters duelling an invisible opponent with a stick. He is Old Martin as an impetuous boy of fifteen.* If you could only imagine what it was like for me at the beginning, to be allowed to serve him. But boys don't dream like that any more – service! Conquest! Riding down Indians in the name of Spain. The inside of my head was one vast plain for feats of daring. I used to lie up in the

I

hayloft for hours reading my Bible – Don Cristobal on the rules of Chivalry. And then he came and made them real. And the only wish of my life is that I had never seen him.

FRANCISCO PIZARRO comes in. He is a man in late middle age: tough, commanding, harsh, wasted, secret. The gestures are blunt and often violent; the expression intense and energetic, capable of fury and cruelty, but also of sudden melancholy and sardonic humour. At the moment he appears more neatly than he is ever to do again: hair and beard are trimmed, and his clothes quite grand, as if he is trying to make a fine impression.

He is accompanied by his Second in Command, HERNANDO DE SOTO, and the Dominican FRAY VINCENTE DE VALVERDE. DE SOTO is an impressive figure in his forties: his whole air breathes an unquestioning loyalty – to his profession, his faith, and to accepted values. He is an admirable soldier and a staunch friend. VALVERDE on the other hand is a peasant Priest whose zeal is not greatly tempered by intelligence, nor sweetened by any anxiety to please.

PIZARRO. I was suckled by a sow. My house is the oldest in Spain – the pig-sty.

OLD MARTIN. He'd made two expeditions to the New World already. Now at over sixty years old he was back in Spain, making one last try. He'd shown the King enough gold to get sole right of discovery in Peru and the title of Viceroy over anything he conquered. In return he was to fit out an army at his own expense. He started recruiting in his own birthplace, Trujillo.

Lights up below as he speaks. Several Spanish villagers have entered, among them SALINAS, a blacksmith, RODAS, a tailor, VASCA, DOMINGO and the CHAVEZ brothers. PIZARRO addresses DIEGO, a young man of twenty-five.

PIZARRO. What's your name?

DIEGO. Diego, sir.

2

PIZARRO. What do you know best?

DIEGO. Horses I suppose, if I was to name anything.

PIZARRO. How would you feel to be Master of Horse, Diego?

DIEGO (*eagerly*). Sir!

PIZARRO. Go over there. Who's smith here?

SALINAS. I am.

PIZARRO. Are you with us?

SALINAS. I'm not against you.

PIZARRO. Who's your friend?

RODAS. Tailor, if it's your business.

PIZARRO. Soldiers never stop mending and patching. They'll be grateful for your assistance.

RODAS. Well find some other fool to give it to them. I'm resting here.

PIZARRO. Rest. (*To* YOUNG MARTIN) Who's this?

DIEGO. Martin Ruiz, sir. A good lad. He knows all his codes of Chivalry by heart. He's aching to be a page, sir.

PIZARRO. How old?

OLD MARTIN. Seventeen.

PIZARRO. Don't lie.

YOUNG MARTIN. Fifteen, sir.

OLD MARTIN *goes off.*

PIZARRO. Parents?

YOUNG MARTIN. Dead, sir.

PIZARRO. Can you write?

YOUNG MARTIN. Two hundred Latin words. Three hundred Spanish.

PIZARRO. Why do you want to come?

YOUNG MARTIN. It's going to be glorious, sir.

PIZARRO. Look you, if you served me you'd be Page to an old slogger: no titles, no traditions. I learnt my trade as a mercenary, going with who best paid me. It's a closed book to me, all that chivalry. But then, not reading or writing, all books are closed to me. If I took you you'd have to be my reader and writer, both.

YOUNG MARTIN. I'd be honoured my Lord. Oh, please my Lord!

PIZARRO. General will do. Let's see your respect. Greet me.

3

(*The boy bows*.) Now to the Church. That's Brother Valverde, our Chaplain.

VALVERDE. The blessing of God on you, my son. And on all who come with us to alter the heathen.

PIZARRO. Now to our Second-in-Command, Cavalier de Soto. I'm sure you all know the Cavalier well by reputation: a great soldier. He has fought under Cordoba! No expedition he seconds can fail. (*He takes a roll of cloth, woven with the design of a llama, from* DE SOTO.) Now look at this! Indian stuff! Ten years ago standing with the great Balboa, I saw a chieftain draw this beast on the leaf of an aloe. And he said to me: Where this roams is uncountable wealth!

RODAS. Oh, yes, uncountable! Ask Sanchez the farrier about that. He listened to talk like that from him five years ago.

DIEGO. Who cares about him?

RODAS. Uncountable bloody wealth? It rained six months and his skin rotted on him. They lost twenty-seven out of fifty.

PIZARRO. And so we may again. What do you think I'm offering? A walk in the country? Jellies and wine in a basket, your hand round your girl? No, I'm promising you swamps. A forest like the beard of the world. Sitting half-buried in earth to escape the mouths of insects. You may live for weeks on palm tree buds and soup made out of leather straps. And at night you will sleep in thick wet darkness with snakes hung over your heads like bell ropes – and black men in that blackness: men that eat each other. And why should you endure all this? Because I believe that beyond this terrible place is a kingdom, where gold is as common as wood is here! I took only two steps in and found cups and pans made out of it solid.

He claps his hands. FELIPILLO *comes in. He is a slim, delicate Indian from Ecuador, loaded with golden ornaments. In actuality* FELIPILLO *is a treacherous and hysterical creature, but at the moment, under his master's eye, he sways forward before the stupefied villagers with a demure grace.*

4

I present Felipillo, captured on my last trip. Look close at his ornaments. To him they are no more than feathers are to us, but they are all gold, my friends. Examine him. Down!

The villagers examine him.

VALVERDE. Look at him well. This is a heathen. A being condemned to eternal flame unless you help him. Don't think we are merely going to destroy his people and lift their wealth. We are going to take from them what they don't value, and give them instead the priceless mercy of heaven. He who helps me lift this dark man into light I absolve of all crimes he ever committed.

PIZARRO. Well?

SALINAS. That's gold right enough.

PIZARRO. And for your taking. I was like you once. Sitting the afternoon away in this same street, drunk in the inn, to bed in the sty. Stink and mud and nothing to look for. Even if you die with me, what's so tender precious to hold you here?

VASCA. You're hissing right!

PIZARRO. I tell you, man: over there you'll be the masters – that'll be your slave.

VASCA. Well, there's a thought: talk about the slave of slaves!

DOMINGO (*timidly*). Do you think it's true?

PIZARRO. Do you say I lie?

DOMINGO. Oh, no, sir . . .

VASCA. Even if he does, what's to keep you here? You're a cooper: how many casks have you made this year? That's no employment for a dog.

PIZARRO. How about you? You're brothers aren't you?

DIEGO. That's the Chavez brothers, Juan and Pedro.

JUAN. Sir.

PEDRO. Sir.

PIZARRO. Well, what d'you say?

JUAN. I say right, sir.

PEDRO. Me too.

VASCA. And me. I'm going to get a slave or two like him.

5

DOMINGO. And me. Vasca's right, you can't do worse than stay here.

RODAS. Well not me, boys. Just you catch Rodas marching through any hissing jungle!

SALINAS. Oh, shut your ape's face. Are you going to sit here for ever and pick fleas? He'll come sir.

PIZARRO. Make your way to Toledo for the muster. Diego, enrol them all and take them along.

DIEGO. Sir!

> YOUNG MARTIN *makes to go off with the rest.*
> PIZARRO *stays him.*

PIZARRO. Boy.

YOUNG MARTIN. Sir.

> *A pause.*

PIZARRO. Master me the names of all officers and men so far listed.

YOUNG MARTIN. Oh, sir! Yes, sir! Thank you, sir!

PIZARRO. You're a page now, so act like one. Dignity at all times.

YOUNG MARTIN (*bowing*). Yes, sir.

PIZARRO. Respect.

YOUNG MARTIN (*bowing*). Yes, sir.

PIZARRO. And obedience.

YOUNG MARTIN (*bowing*). Yes, sir.

PIZARRO. And it isn't necessary to salute every ten seconds.

YOUNG MARTIN (*bowing*). No, sir.

VALVERDE. Come, my son, there's work to do.

> *They go off.*

PIZARRO. Strange sight, yourself, just as you were in this very street.

DE SOTO. Do you like it?

PIZARRO. No, I was a fool. Dreamers deserve what they get.

DE SOTO. And what are you dreaming about now?

PIZARRO. Gold.

DE SOTO. Oh, come. Gold is not enough lodestone for you, not any more to drag you back to the new world.

PIZARRO. You're right. At my age things become what they really are. Gold turns into metal.

DE SOTO. Then why? You could stay here now and be hero for a province. What's left to endure so much for – especially with your infirmity? You've earned the right to comfort. Your country would gladly grant it to you for the rest of your life.

PIZARRO. My country, where is that?

DE SOTO. Spain, sir.

PIZARRO. Spain and I have been strangers since I was a boy. The only spot I know in it is here – this filthy village. This is Spain to me. Is this where you wish me comfort? For twenty-two years I drove pigs down this street because my father couldn't own to my mother. Twenty-two years without one single day of hope. When I turned soldier and dragged my arquebus along the roads of Italy, I was so famished I was beyond eating. I got nothing and I gave nothing, and though I groaned for that once I'm glad with it now. Because I owe nothing . . . Once the world could have had me for a petty farm, two rocky fields and a Senor to my name. It said 'No'. Ten years on it could have had me for double – small estate, fifty oranges and a Sir to them. It said 'No'. Twenty years more and it could still have had me cheap: Balboa's trusty lieutenant, marched with him into the Pacific and claimed it for Spain: State Pension and dinner once a week with the local Mayor. But the world said 'No'. Said 'No' and said 'No'. Well, now it's going to know me. If I live this next year I'm going to get a name that won't ever be forgotten. A name to be sung here for centuries in your ballads, out there under the cork trees where I sat as a boy with bandages for shoes. I amuse you.

DE SOTO. Surely you see you don't.

PIZARRO. Oh, yes, I amuse you Cavalier de Soto. The old pigherd lumbering after fame. You inherited your honour – I had to root for mine like the pigs. It's amusing.

7

II

Lights whiter, colder.

He kneels. An organ sounds: the austere polyphony of Spanish celebration. VALVERDE *enters, bearing an immense wooden Christ. He is accompanied by his assistant,* FRAY MARCOS DE NIZZA, *a Franciscan, a man of far more serene temper and intellectual maturity. All the villagers come in also, wearing the white cloaks of chivalry and carrying banners. Among them is* PEDRO DE CANDIA, *a Venetian captain, wearing a pearl in one ear and walking with a lazy stealth that at once suggests danger.* OLD MARTIN *comes in.*

OLD MARTIN. On the day of St John the Evangelist, our weapons were consecrated in the Cathedral Church of Panama. Our muster was one hundred and eighty-seven, with horses for twenty-seven.

VALVERDE. You are the huntsmen of God. The weapons you draw are sacred! Oh, God, invest us all with the courage of Thy unflinching Son. Show us our way to beat the savage out of his dark forests on to the broad plain of Thy Grace.

DE NIZZA. And comfort, we pray, all warriors that shall be in affliction from this setting out.

OLD MARTIN. Fray Marcos de Nizza, Franciscan, appointed to assist Valverde.

DE NIZZA. You are the bringers of food to starving peoples. You go to break mercy with them like bread, and outpour gentleness into their cups. You will lay before them the inexhaustible table of free spirit, and invite to it all who have dieted on terror. You will bring to all tribes the nourishment of pity. You will sow their fields with love, and teach them to harvest the crop of it, each yield in its season. Remember this always: we are their New World.

VALVERDE. Approach all and be blessed.

During this, the men kneel and are blessed.

OLD MARTIN. Pedro de Candia, Cavalier from Venice, in

8

charge of weapons and artillery. These villagers you know already. There were many others of course. Almagro, the General's partner, who stayed to organize reinforcements and follow in three months. Riquelme the Treasurer. Pedro of Ayala and Blas of Atienza. Herrada the Swordsman and Gonzales of Toledo. And Juan de Barbaran whom everyone called the good servant out of love for him. And many smaller men. Even its youngest member saw himself with a following of Indians and a province for an orchard. It was a tumbled company, none too noble but ginger for wealth.

Enter E S T E T E : *a stiff, haughty man, dressed in the black of the Spanish court.*

And chiefly there was—

E S T E T E . Miguel Estete. Royal Veedor, and Overseer in the name of King Carlos the Fifth. You should not have allowed anyone to be blessed before me.

P I Z A R R O . Your pardon, Veedor, I don't understand affairs of before and after.

E S T E T E . That is evident. General, on this expedition my name is the law: it is spoken with the King's authority.

P I Z A R R O . Your pardon, but on this expedition my name is the law: there will be no other.

E S T E T E . In matters military.

P I Z A R R O . In all matters.

E S T E T E . In all that do not infringe the majesty of the King.

P I Z A R R O . What matters could?

E S T E T E . Remember your duty to God, sir, and to the throne, sir, and you will not discover them.

P I Z A R R O (*furious*). De Soto! In the name of Spain our holy country, I invest you as second in Command to me. Subject only to me. In the name of Spain our Holy country – I – I –. (*He falters, clutching his side in pain. A pause. The men whisper among themselves*) Take the banners out . . .

D E S O T O . Take up your banners. March!

The organ music continues: all march out leaving P I Z A R R O *and his* P A G E *alone on the stage. Only*

9

when all the rest are gone does the General collapse. The boy is frightened and concerned.

YOUNG MARTIN. What is it, sir?

PIZARRO. A wound from long ago. A knife to the bone. A savage put it into me for life. It troubles me at times . . . You'll start long before me with your wounds. With your killing too. I wonder how you'll like that.

YOUNG MARTIN. You watch me, sir.

PIZARRO. I will. You deal in deaths when you are a soldier, and all your study should be to make them clean, what scratches kill and how to cut them.

YOUNG MARTIN. But surely, sir, there's more to soldiering than that?

PIZARRO. You mean, honour, glory – traditions of the service?

YOUNG MARTIN. Yes, sir.

PIZARRO. Dungballs. Soldiers are for killing: that's their reason.

YOUNG MARTIN. But, sir –

PIZARRO. What?

YOUNG MARTIN. It's not just killing.

PIZARRO. Look, boy: know something. Men cannot just stand as men in this world. It's too big for them and they grow scared. So they build themselves shelters against the bigness, do you see? They call the shelters Court, Army, Church. They're useful against loneliness, Martin, but they're not true. They're not real, Martin, Do you see?

YOUNG MARTIN. No, sir. Not truthfully sir . . .

PIZARRO. No, sir. Not truthfully sir! Why must you be so young? Look at you. Only a quarter formed. A colt the world will break for its sightless track. Listen once. Army loyalty is blasphemy. The world of soldiers is a yard of ungrowable children. They play with ribbons and make up ceremonies just to keep out the rest of the world. They add up the number of their blue dead and their green dead and call that their history. But all this is just the flower the bandit carves on his knife before shoving it into a man's side . . . What's Army Tradition? Nothing but years of Us against Them. Christ-men against Pagan-men. Men against men. I've had a life of it boy, and let me tell you it's nothing but a nightmare game, played by brutes to give themselves a reason.

YOUNG MARTIN. But sir, a noble reason can make a fight glorious.

PIZARRO. Give me a reason that stays noble once you start hacking off limbs in its name. There isn't a cause in the world to set against this pain. Noble's a word. Leave it for the books.

YOUNG MARTIN. I can't believe that, sir.

PIZARRO. Look at you – hope, lovely hope, it's on you like dew. Do you know where you're going? Into the forest. A hundred miles of dark and screaming. The dark we all came out of, hot. Things flying, fleeing, falling dead – and their death unnoticed. Take your noble reasons there, Martin. Pitch your silk flags in that black and wave your crosses at the wild cats. See what awe they command. Be advised, boy. Go back to Spain.

YOUNG MARTIN. No, sir. I'm coming with you. I can learn, sir.

PIZARRO. You will be taught. Not by me. The forest.

He stumps out.

III

The boy is left alone. The stage darkens and the huge medallion high on the back wall begins to glow. Great cries of 'Inca!' are heard. The boy bolts off stage. Exotic music mixes with the chanting. Slowly the medallion opens outwards to form a huge golden sun with twelve great rays. In the centre stands ATAHUALLPA, *sovereign Inca of Peru, masked, crowned, and dressed in gold. When he speaks, his voice, like the voices of all the Incas, is strangely formalized.*

Enter below the Inca court: VILLAC UMU, *the High Priest,* CHALLCUCHIMA, MANCO *and others, all masked, and robed in terracotta. They prostrate themselves.*

C   II

MANCO. Atahuallpa! God!

ATAHUALLPA. God hears.

MANCO. Manco your Chasqui speaks. I bring truth from many runners what has been seen in the Farthest Province. White men sitting on huge sheep. The sheep are red! Everywhere their leader shouts aloud 'Here is God!'

ATAHUALLPA. The White God!

VILLAC UMU. Beware, beware Inca!

ATAHUALLPA. All-powerful spirit who left this place before my ancestors ruled you. The White God returns!

CHALLCUCHIMA. You do not know this.

ATAHUALLPA. He has been long waited for. If he comes, it is with blessing. Then my people will see I did well to take the Crown.

VILLAC UMU. Ware you! Your mother Moon wears a veil of green fire. An eagle fell on to the temple in Cuzco.

MANCO. It is true, Capac. He fell out of the sky.

VILLAC UMU. Out of a green sky.

CHALLCUCHIMA. On to a house of gold.

VILLAC UMU. When the world ends, small birds grow sharp claws.

ATAHUALLPA. Cover your mouth. (*All cover their mouths*). If the White God comes to bless me, all must see him.

The Court retires. ATAHUALLPA *remains on stage, motionless in his sunflower. He stays in this position until the end of Scene VII.*

IV

Mottled light.

Province of Tumbez. Screams and whoops of alarm imitating tropical bird cries. A horde of Indians rushes across the stage pursued by soldiers.

DE CANDIA. Grab that one! That's the chief.

12

They capture the Chieftain. At the sight of this, all the Indians fall silent and passive. DE CANDIA *approaches him with drawn sword.*

Now, you brownie bastard, show us gold.

PIZARRO. Gently, De Candia. You'll get nothing from him in terror.

DE CANDIA. Let's see.

PIZARRO. God's wounds! Put up! Felipillo, ask for gold.

FELIPILLO *adopts a set of stylized gestures for his interpreting, in the manner of sign language.*

CHIEF. We have no gold. All was taken by the great King in his war.

PIZARRO. What King?

CHIEF. Holy Atahuallpa, Inca of earth and sky. His Kingdom is the widest in the world.

DE SOTO. How wide?

CHIEF. A man can run in it every day for a year.

DE SOTO. More than a thousand miles.

ESTETE. Poor savage, trying to impress us with his little tribe.

PIZARRO. I think we've found more than a little tribe, Veedor. Tell me of this King. Who did he fight?

CHIEF. His brother Huascar. His father the great Inca Huayana grew two sons. One by a wife, one by a not-wife. At his death he cut the Kingdom in two for them. But Atahuallpa wanted all. So he made war, and killed his brother. Now he is lord of earth and sky.

PIZARRO. And he's the bastard?

All the INDIANS *cry out.*

Answer! He's the bastard?

CHIEF. He is Son of the Sun. He needs no wedded mother. He is God.

INDIANS (*chanting*). Sapa Inca! Inca Capac!

PIZARRO. God?

CHIEF. God.

PIZARRO. God on earth?

VALVERDE. Christ defend us!

DE SOTO. Do you believe this?

13

CHIEF. It is true. The sun is God. Atahuallpa is his child sent to shine on us for a few years of life. Then he will return to his father's palace and live for ever.

PIZARRO. God on earth!

VALVERDE. Oh, my brothers, where have we come? The land of Anti-Christ! Do your duty, Spaniards! Take each an Indian and work to shift his soul. Go to them. Show them rigour! No softness to gentle idolatry. (*To the* INDIANS) The cross, you pagan dust!

They try to escape.

Stay them!

The SPANIARDS *ring them with swords.*

Repeat. Jesus Christ Inca!

INDIANS (*uncertainly*). Jesus Christ Inca!

ESTETE. Jesus Christ Inca!

INDIANS. Jesus Christ Inca!

The soldiers herd them off stage. Their cries punctuate the end of the scene. All go off after them, save PIZARRO *and* DE SOTO.

ATAHUALLPA. He surely is a god. He teaches my people to praise him.

PIZARRO. He's a god all right. They're scared to hell of him. And a bastard too. That's civil war – bastards against bastards!

ATAHUALLPA. I will see him. Let no one harm these men.

PIZARRO. Let's see you, then. What's it look like to be Son of the Sun?

DE SOTO. That's something in Europe no one's ever dared call himself.

PIZARRO. God on earth, living for ever!

DE SOTO. He's got a shock coming.

He goes off.

PIZARRO. Do you hear that, God? You're not going to like that! Because we've got a god worth a thousand of yours. A gentle God with gentle priests, and a couple of big cannon to blow you out of the sky!

VALVERDE (*off*) Jesus Christ Inca!

PIZARRO. Christ the Merciful, with his shackles and stakes!

14

So enjoy yourself while you can. Have a glorious shine.
(*He makes the sign of the cross*). Take that, Anti-Christ!
He runs off, laughing.

VALVERDE (*off*). Jesus Christ Inca!

INDIANS (*off*) *Cry out.*

Enter VILLAC UMU *and* CHALLCUCHIMA.

VILLAC UMU. Your people groan.

ATAHUALLPA. They groan with my voice.

CHALLCUCHIMA. Your people weep.

ATAHUALLPA. They weep with my tears.

CHALLCUCHIMA. He searches all the houses. He seeks
your crown. Remember the prophecy! The twelfth Lord
of the Four Quarters shall be the last. Inca, ware you!

VILLAC UMU. Inca, ware you!

ATAHUALLPA (*To* CHALLCUCHIMA) Go to him. Take
him my word. Tell him to greet me at Cajamarca, behind
the great mountains. If he is a god he will find me. If he
is no god, he will die.

Lights down on him. Priest and noblemen retire.

V

Night. Wild bird cries. DOMINGO *and* VASCA *on sentry
duty.*

VASCA. There must be a hissing thousand of 'em, every
night we halt.

DOMINGO. Why don't they just come and get us?

VASCA. They're waiting.

DOMINGO. What for?

VASCA. Maybe they're cannibals and there's a feast day
coming up.

DOMINGO. Very funny . . . Six weeks in this hissing forest
and not one smell of gold. I think we've been had.

VASKA. Unless they're hiding it, like the General says.

DOMINGO. I don't believe it. God damned place. I'm starting
to rust.

15

VASCA. We all are. It's the damp. Another week and we'll have to get the blacksmith to cut us out.

Enter ESTETE *with* DE CANDIA *carrying an arquebus.*

VASCA. Who's there?

DE CANDIA. Talk on duty again and *I'll* cut you out.

DOMINGO. Yes, sir.

VASCA. Yes, sir.

They separate and go off.

DE CANDIA. They're right. Everything's rusting. Even you, my darling. (*The gun*) Look at her, Strozzi's most perfect model. She can stop a horse at five hundred paces. You're too good for brownies, my sweet.

ESTETE. What are they waiting for? Why don't they just attack and be done with it?

DE CANDIA. They'd find nothing against them. A hundred and eighty terrified men, nine of these and two cannon. If your King wasn't so mean we might just stand a chance out here.

ESTETE. Hold your tongue, De Candia.

DE CANDIA. Good: loyalty. That's what I like to see. The only thing that puzzles me is what the hell you get out of it. They tell me Royal Overseers get nothing.

ESTETE. Any man without self-interest must puzzle a Venetian. If you serve a King you must kill personal ambition. Only then can you become a channel between the people and its collective glory – which otherwise it would never feel. In Byzantium Court Officials were castrated to resemble the Order of Angels. But I don't expect you to understand.

DE CANDIA. You Spaniards! You men with missions! You just can't bear to think of yourselves as the thieves you are.

ESTETE. How dare you, sir!

Enter PIZARRO *and* YOUNG MARTIN.

DE CANDIA. Our noble General. They say in the Indies he traded his immortal part to the Devil.

ESTETE. For what, pray? Health? Breeding? Handsomeness?

16

DE CANDIA. That they don't tell.

ESTETE. I daresay not. I only wonder His Majesty could give command to such a man. I believe he's mad.

DE CANDIA. No, but still dangerous.

ESTETE. What do you mean?

DE CANDIA. I've served under many men: but this is the first who makes me afraid. Look into him and you'll see a kind of death.

Bird cries fill the forest.

PIZARRO. Listen to them. That's the world. The eagle rips the condor; the condor rips the crow. And the crow would blind all the eagles in the sky if once it had the beak to do it. The clothed hunt the naked; the legitimates hunt the bastards, and put down the word Gentlemen to blot up the blood. Your Chivalry rules don't govern me, Martin. They're for belonging birds – like them: legitimate birds with claws trim on the perch their feathers left to them. Make no error; if I could once peck them off it, I'd tear them into gobbets to feed cats. Don't ever trust me, boy.

YOUNG MARTIN. Sir? I'm your man.

PIZARRO. Don't ever trust me.

YOUNG MARTIN. Sir?

PIZARRO. Or if you must, never say I deceived you. Know me.

YOUNG MARTIN. I do, sir. You are all I ever want to be.

PIZARRO. I am nothing you could ever want to be, or any man alive. Believe this: if the time ever came for you to harry me, I'd rip you too, easy as look at you. Because you belong too, Martin.

YOUNG MARTIN. I belong to you, sir!

PIZARRO. You belong to hope. To faith. To priests and pretences. To dipping flags and ducking heads; to laying hands and licking rings; to powers and parchments; and the whole vast stupid congregation of crowners and cross-kissers. You're a worshipper. Martin. A groveller. You were born with feet but you prefer your knees. It's you who make Bishops – Kings – Generals. You trust me, I'll hurt you past believing. (*A pause*) Have the sentries changed?

YOUNG MARTIN. Not yet, sir.

PIZARRO. Little Lord of Hope, I'm harsh with you. You own everything I've lost. I despise the keeping, and I loathe the losing. Where can a man live, between two hates?

He goes towards the two officers.

Gentlemen.

ESTETE. How is your wound tonight, General?

PIZARRO. The calmer for your inquiring, Veedor.

DE CANDIA. Well, and what's your plan, sir?

PIZARRO. To go on until I'm stopped.

DE CANDIA. Admirable simplicity.

ESTETE. What kind of plan is that?

PIZARRO. You have a better? It's obvious they've been ordered to hold off.

ESTETE. Why?

PIZARRO. If it's wickedness I'm sure the crown can guess it as soon as the Army.

ESTETE. Sir, I know your birth hasn't fitted for much civility, but remember, in me speaks your King.

PIZARRO. Well, go and write to him. Set down more about my unfitness in your report. Then show it to the birds.

He goes off. ESTETE *goes off another way.* DE CANDIA *laughs and follows him.*

VI

Light brightens to morning.
Enter OLD MARTIN.

OLD MARTIN. We were in the forest for six weeks, but at last we escaped and found on the other side our first witness of a great empire. There was a road fifteen feet wide, bordered with mimosa and blue glories, with walls on both sides the height of a man. We rode it for days, six horses abreast: and all the way, far up the hillsides, were huge fields of corn laid out in terraces, and a net of water in a thousand canals. (*Exit*)

Lights up on ATAHUALLPA, *above.*

MANCO. Manco your Chasqui speaks. They move on the road to Ricaplaya.

ATAHUALLPA. What do they do?

MANCO. They walk through the field terraces. They listen to toil-songs. They clap their hands at fields of llama.

Enter groups of INDIANS, *singing a toil-song and miming their work of sowing and reaping.* PIZARRO, *the* PRIESTS, FELIPILLO *and* SOLDIERS, *among them* DE SOTO, DE CANDIA, DIEGO, ESTETE *and* YOUNG MARTIN, *enter and stand watching.* YOUNG MARTIN *carries a drum.*

DE NIZZA. How beautiful their tongue sounds.

YOUNG MARTIN. I'm trying to study it but it's very hard. All the words seem to slip together.

FELIPILLO. Oh, very hard, yes. But more hard for Indian to learn Spanish.

DE NIZZA. I'm sure. See how contented they look.

DIEGO. It's the first time I've ever seen people glad at working.

DE SOTO. This is their Headman.

PIZARRO. You are the Lord of the Manor?

FELIPILLO *interprets.*

HEADMAN. Here all work together in families: fifty, a hundred, a thousand. I am head of a thousand families. I give out to all food. I give out to all clothes. I give out to all confessing.

DE NIZZA. Confessing?

HEADMAN. I have priest power . . . I confess my people of all crimes against the laws of the sun.

DE NIZZA. What laws are these?

HEADMAN. It is the seventh month. That is why they must pick corn.

ATAHUALLPA (*intoning*) In the eighth month you will plough. In the ninth, sow maize. In the tenth, mend your roofs.

19

HEADMAN. Each age also has its tasks.

ATAHUALLPA. Nine years to twelve, protect harvests. Twelve to eighteen, care for herds. Eighteen to twenty-five, warriors for me – Atahuallpa Inca!

FELIPILLO. They are stupid; always do what they are told.

DE SOTO. This is because they are poor?

FELIPILLO. Not poor. Not rich. All same.

ATAHUALLPA. At twenty-five all will marry. All will receive one tupu of land.

HEADMAN. What may be covered by one hundred pounds of maize.

ATAHUALLPA. They will never move from there. At birth of a son one more tupu will be given. At birth of a daughter, half a tupu. At fifty all people will leave work for ever and be fed in honour till they die.

DE SOTO. I have settled several lands. This is the first I've entered which shames our Spain.

ESTETE. Shames?

PIZARRO. Oh, it's not difficult to shame Spain. Here shames every country which teaches we are born greedy for possessions. Clearly we're made greedy when we're assured it's natural. But there's a picture for a Spanish eye! There's nothing to covet, so covetousness dies at birth.

DE SOTO. But don't you have any nobles or grand people?

HEADMAN. The King has great men near him to order the country. But they are few.

DE SOTO. How then can he make sure so many are happy over so large a land?

HEADMAN. His messengers run light and dark, one after one, over four great roads. No one else may move on them. So he has eyes everywhere. He sees you now.

PIZARRO. Now?

ATAHUALLPA. Now!

CHALLCUCHIMA *enters with* MANCO, *bearing the image of the Sun on a pole.*

CHALLCUCHIMA. I bring greeting from Atahuallpa Inca, Lord of the Four Quarters, King of the earth and sky.

ESTETE. I will speak with him. A King's man must always

greet a King's man. We bring greeting from King Carlos, Emperor of Spain and Austria. We bring blessing from Jesus Christ, the Son of God.

ATAHUALLPA. Blessing!

CHALLCUCHIMA. *I* am sent by the son of God. He orders *you* to visit him.

ESTETE. Orders? Does he take us for servants?

CHALLCUCHIMA. All men are his servants.

ESTETE. Does he think so? He's got awakening coming.

CHALLCUCHIMA. Awakening?

PIZARRO. Veedor, under pardon, let my peasant tongue have a word. Where is your King?

CHALLCUCHIMA. Cajamarca. Behind the great mountains. Perhaps they are too high for you.

ESTETE. There isn't a hill in your whole country a Spaniard couldn't climb in full armour.

CHALLCUCHIMA. That is wonderful.

PIZARRO. How long should we march before we find him?

CHALLCUCHIMA. One life of Mother Moon.

FELIPILLO. A month.

PIZARRO. For us, two weeks. Tell him we come.

ATAHUALLPA. He gives his word with no fear.

CHALLCUCHIMA. Ware you! It is great danger to take back your word.

PIZARRO. I do not fear danger. What I say I do.

CHALLCUCHIMA. So. Do.

  CHALLCUCHIMA *and* MANCO *go off*.

ATAHUALLPA. He speaks with a God's tongue. Let us take his blessing.

DE SOTO. Well, God help us now.

DE CANDIA. He'd better. I don't know who else will get us out of this. Certainly not the artillery.

FELIPILLO (*imitating* CHALCUCHIMA'S *walk and voice*). So! Do.

DE SOTO. Be still. You're too free.

ESTETE. My advice to you now is to wait for the reinforcements.

PIZARRO. I thank you for it.

DE SOTO. There's no telling when they'll come, sir. We daren't stay till then.

PIZARRO. But *you* of course will.

ESTETE. I?

PIZARRO. I cannot hazard the life of a Royal officer.

ESTETE. My personal safety has never concerned me, General. My Master's service is all I care for.

PIZARRO. That's why we must ensure its continuance. I'll give you twenty men. You can make a garrison.

ESTETE. I must decline, General. If you go – I go also.

PIZARRO. I'm infinitely moved, Veedor – but my orders remain. You stay here. (*To his page*) Call Assembly.

YOUNG MARTIN (*banging his drum*). Assembly! Assembly!

VII

The Company pelts on. ESTETE *goes off angrily.*

PIZARRO. We are commanded to court by a brown King, more powerful than any you have ever heard of, sole owner of all the gold we came for. We have three roads. Go back, and he kills us. Stay here, and he kills us. Go on, and he still may kill us. Who fears to meet him can stay here with the Veedor and swell a garrison. He'll have no disgrace, but no gold neither. Who stirs?

RODAS. Well, I hissing stir for once. I'm not going to be chewed up by no bloody heathen king. What do you say, Vasca lad?

VASCA. I don't know. I reckon if he chews us first, he chews you second. We're the eggs and you're the stew.

RODAS. Ha, ha, day of a hundred jokes!

SALINAS. Come on friend, for God's sake. Who's going to sew us up if you desert?

RODAS. You can all rot for all I care, breeches and what's bloody in 'em.

SALINAS. Bastard!

RODAS. To hell with the lot. of you! (*He walks off*)

PIZARRO. Anyone else?

DOMINGO. Well, I don't know . . . Maybe he's right.

JUAN. Hey, Pedro, what do you think?

PEDRO. Hell, no! Vasca's right. It's as safe to go as stay here.

SALINAS. That's right.

VASCA. Anyway, I didn't come to keep no hissing garrison.

PEDRO. Nor me. I'm going on.

JUAN. Right boy.

SALINAS. And me.

DOMINGO. Well, I don't know . . .

VASCA. Oh, close your mouth. You're like a hissing girl. (*To* PIZARRO.) We're coming. Just find us the gold.

PIZARRO. All right then. (*To* YOUNG MARTIN) You stay here.

YOUNG MARTIN. No, sir. The place of a squire is at all times by his Knight's side. Laws of Chivalry.

PIZARRO (*touched*). Get them in rank. *Move!*

YOUNG MARTIN. Company in rank. Move!

The soldiers form up in rank.

PIZARRO. Stand firm. Firmer! . . . Look at you, you could be dead already. If he sees you like that you will be. Make no error, he's watching every step you take. You're not men any longer, you're Gods now. Eternal Gods, each one of you. Two can play this immortality game, my lads. I want to see you move over his land like figures from a Lent Procession. He must see Gods walk on earth. Indifferent! Uncrushable! No death to be afraid of. I tell you, one shiver dooms the lot of us. One yelp of fright and we'll never be heard of again. He'll serve us like cheeseworms you crush with a knife. So come on you tattered trash – shake out the straw. Forget your village magic: fingers in crosses, saints under your shirts. You can grant prayers now – no need to answer them. Come on! Fix your eyes! Follow the pig-boy to his glory! I'll have an Empire for my farm. A million boys driving in the pigs at night. And each one of you will own a share – juicy black earth a hundred mile apiece – and golden ploughs to cut it! Get up you God-boys – March!

23

MARTIN *bangs his drum. The Spaniards begin to march in slow motion. Above, masked Indians move on to the upper level.*

MANCO. They move Inca! they come! One hundred and sixty and seven.

ATAHUALLPA. Where?

MANCO. Zaran.

VILLAC UMU. Ware! Ware, Inca!

MANCO. They move all in step. Not fast, not slow. They keep straight on from dark to dark.

VILLAC UMU. Ware! Ware, Inca.

MANCO. They are at Motupe, Inca! They do not look on left or right.

VILLAC UMU. Ware! this is great danger.

ATAHUALLPA. No danger. He is coming to bless me. A god and all his priests. Praise Father Sun!

ALL ABOVE (*chanting*). Viracochian Aticsi.

ATAHUALLPA. Praise Sapa Inca!

ALL ABOVE. Sapa Inca! Sapa Inca!

ATAHUALLPA. Praise Inti Cori.

ALL ABOVE. Caylla int'i cori.

CHALLCUCHIMA. They come to the mountains.

VILLAC UMU. Kill them now.

ATAHUALLPA. Praise Atahuallpa.

VILLAC UMU. Destroy them! Teach them death!

ATAHUALLPA. Praise Atahuallpa!

ALL ABOVE. Atahuallpa! Sapa Inca! Huaccha Cuyak!

ATAHUALLPA. Let them see my mountains!

A crash of primitive instruments. The lights snap out and, lit from the side, the rays of the metal sun throw long shadows across the wooden wall. All the Spaniards fall down. A cold blue light fills the stage.

DE SOTO. God in heaven!

Enter OLD MARTIN.

OLD MARTIN. You call them the Andes. Picture a curtain of stone hung by some giant across your path. Mountains set on mountains: cliffs on cliffs. Hands of rock a hundred yards high, with flashing nails where the snow never moved, scratching the gashed face of the sun. For miles around the jungle lay black in its shadow. A freezing cold fell on us.

PIZARRO. Up, my godlings. Up, my little gods. Take heart, now. He's watching you. *Get to your feet!* (*To* DIEGO) Master, what of the horses?

DIEGO. D'you need them sir?

PIZARRO. They're vital, boy.

DIEGO. Then you'll have 'em, sir. They'll follow you as we will.

PIZARRO. Up we go, then! We're coming for you, Atahuallpa. Show me the toppest peak-top you can pile – show me the lid of the world – I'll stand tiptoe on it and pull you right out of the sky. I'll grab you by the legs, you Son of the Sun, and smash your flaming crown on the rocks. Bless them, Church!

VALVERDE. God stay you, and stay with you all.

DE NIZZA. Amen.

Whilst PIZARRO *is calling his last speech to the Inca, the silent King thrice beckons to him, and retires backwards out of the sun into blackness. In the cold light there now ensues:*

VIII

THE MIME OF THE GREAT ASCENT

As OLD MARTIN *describes their ordeal, the men climb the Andes. It is a terrible progress; a stumbling, tortuous climb into the clouds, over ledges and giant chasms, performed to an eerie, cold music made from the thin whine of huge saws.*

OLD MARTIN. Have you ever climbed a mountain in full armour? That's what we did, him going first the whole way up a tiny path into the clouds, with drops sheer on both sides into nothing. For hours we crept forward like blind men, the sweat freezing on our faces, lugging skittery leaking horses, and pricked all the time for the ambush that would tip us into death. Each turn of the path it grew colder. The friendly trees of the forest dropped away, and there were only pines. Then they went too, and there were just scrubby little bushes standing up in ice. All round us the rocks began to whine with cold. And always above us, or below us, those filthy condor birds, hanging on the air with great tasselled wings.

It grows darker. The music grows colder yet. The men freeze and hang their heads for a long moment, before resuming their desperate climb.

Then night. We lay down twos and threes together on the path, and hugged like lovers for warmth in that burning cold. And most cried. We got up with cold iron for bones and went on. Four days like that: groaning, not speaking; the breath a blade in our lungs. Four days, slowly, like flies on a wall; limping flies, dying flies, up an endless wall of rock. A tiny army lost in the creases of the moon.

INDIANS (*off: in echo*). Stand!

The Spaniards whirl round. VILLAC UMU *and his attendants appear, clothed entirely in white fur. The High Priest wears a snow-white llama head on top of his own.*

VILLAC UMU. You see Villac Umu. Chief Priest of the Sun. Why do you come?

PIZARRO. To see the Great Inca.

VILLAC UMU. Why will you see him?

PIZARRO. To give him blessing.

VILLAC UMU. Why will you bless him?

PIZARRO. He is a God. I am a God.

VALVERDE (*sotto voce*). General!

PIZARRO. Be still.

VILLAC UMU. Below you is the town of Cajamarca. The great Inca orders: rest there. Tomorrow early he will come to you. Do not move from the town. Outside it is his anger.

He goes off with his attendants.

VALVERDE. What have you done, sir?

PIZARRO. Sent him news to amaze him.

VALVERDE. I cannot approve blasphemy.

PIZARRO. To conquer for Christ, one can surely usurp his name for a night, Father. Set on.

IX

A dreary light.
The Spaniards fan out over the stage. DE SOTO *goes off.*

OLD MARTIN. So down we went from ledge to ledge, and out on to a huge plain of eucalyptus trees, all glowing in the failing light. And there, at the other end, lay a vast white town with roofs of straw. As night fell, we entered it. We came into an empty square, larger than any in Spain. All round it ran long white buildings, three times the height of a man. Everywhere was grave quiet. You could almost touch the silence. Up on the hill we could see the Inca's tents, and the lights from his fires ringing the valley. (*Exit.*)
Some sit. All look up at the hillside.

DIEGO. How many do you reckon there's up there?

DE CANDIA. Ten thousand.

DE SOTO (*re-entering*). The town's empty. Not even a dog.

DOMINGO. It's a trap. I know it's a trap.

PIZARRO. Felipillo! Where's that little rat? Felipillo!

FELIPILLO. General, Lord.

PIZARRO. What does this mean?

FELIPILLO. I don't know. Perhaps it is order of welcome. Great people. Much honour.

VALVERDE. Nonsense, it's a trick, a brownie trick. He's got us all marked for death.

DE NIZZA. He could have killed us at any time. Why should he take such trouble with us?

PIZARRO. Because we're Gods, Father. He'll change soon enough when he finds out different.

DE SOTO. Brace up, boy! It's what you came for, isn't it? Death and glory?

YOUNG MARTIN. Yes, sir.

PIZARRO. De Soto. De Candia. (*They go to him*) It's got to be ambush. That's our only hope.

DE SOTO. Round the square?

PIZARRO. Lowers the odds. Three thousand at most.

DE CANDIA. Thirty to one. Not low enough.

PIZARRO. It'll have to do. We're not fighting ten thousand or three. One man: that's all. Get him, the rest collapse.

DE SOTO. Even if we can, they'll kill us all to get him back.

PIZARRO. If there's a knife at his throat? It's a risk, sure. But what do worshippers do when you snatch their God?

DE CANDIA. Pray to you instead.

DIEGO. It's wonderful. Grab the King, grab the Kingdom!

DE NIZZA. It would avoid bloodshed.

PIZARRO. What do you say?

DE CANDIA. It's the only way. It could work.

DE SOTO. With God's help.

PIZARRO. Then pray all. Disperse. Light fires. Make confession. Battle orders at first light.

Most disperse. Some lie down to pray and sleep.

DE NIZZA (*to* DE CANDIA). Shall I hear your confession now, my son?

DE CANDIA. You'd best save all that for tomorrow, Father. For the men who are left. What have we got to confess tonight but thoughts of murder?

DE NIZZA. Then confess those.

DE CANDIA. Why? Should I feel shame for them? What would I say to God if I refused to destroy His enemies?

VALVERDE. More Venetian nonsense!

DE NIZZA. God has no enemies, my son. Only those nearer to Him or farther from Him.

DE CANDIA. Well, my job is to aim at the far ones. I'll go and position the guns. Excuse me.

He goes off.

PIZARRO. Diego, look to the horses. I know they're sorry, but we'll need them brisk.

VALVERDE. Come my brother, we'll pray together.

They go too.

PIZARRO. The cavalry will split and hide in the buildings, there and there.

DE SOTO. And the infantry in file – there, and round there.

PIZARRO. Perfect. Herrada can command one flank, de Barbaran the other. Everyone hidden.

DE SOTO. They'll suspect then.

PIZARRO. No, the Church will greet them.

DE SOTO. We'll need a watchword.

PIZARRO. San Jago.

DE SOTO. San Jago. Good.

The old man comes upon his page, who is sitting huddled by himself.

PIZARRO. Are you scared?

YOUNG MARTIN. No, sir. Yes, sir.

PIZARRO. You're a good boy. If ever we get out of this, I'll make you a gift of whatever you ask me. Is that chivalrous enough for you?

YOUNG MARTIN. Being your page is enough, sir.

PIZARRO. And there's nothing else you want?

YOUNG MARTIN. A sword, sir.

PIZARRO. Of course . . . Take what rest you can. Call Assembly at first light.

YOUNG MARTIN. Yes, sir. Good night sir.

DE SOTO. Good night, Martin. Try and sleep.

The boy lies down to sleep. The singing of prayers is heard, off, all around.

PIZARRO. Hope, lovely hope. A sword's no mere bar of metal for him. His world still has sacred objects. How remote . . .

DIEGO. Holy Virgin, give us victory. If you do, I'll make you a present of a fine Indian cloak. But you let us down, and I'll leave you for the Virgin of the Conception, and I mean that.

He lies down also. The prayers die away. Silence.

X

Semi-darkness.

PIZARRO. This is probably our last night. If we die, what will we have gone for?

DE SOTO. Spain. Christ.

PIZARRO. I envy you, Cavalier.

DE SOTO. For what?

PIZARRO. Your service. God. King. It's all simple for you.

DE SOTO. No, sir, it's not simple. But it's what I've chosen.

PIZARRO. Yes. And what have I chosen?

DE SOTO. To be a King yourself. Or as good, if we win here.

PIZARRO. And what's that at my age? Not only swords turn into bars of metal. Sceptres too. What's left, De Soto?

DE SOTO. What you told me in Spain. A name for ballads. The man of Honour has three good lives: The Life Today. The Life to Come. The Life of Fame.

PIZARRO. Fame is long. Death is longer . . . Does anyone ever die for anything? I thought so once. Life was fierce with feeling. It was all hope, like on that boy. Swords shone and armour sang, and cheese bit you, and kissing burned and Death – ah, death was going to make an exception in my case. I couldn't believe I was ever going to die. But once you know it – really know it – it's all over. You know you've been cheated, and nothing's the same again.

DE SOTO. Cheated?

PIZARRO. Time cheats us all the way. Children, yes – having children goes some steps to defeating it. Nothing else. It would have been good to have a son.

DE SOTO. Did you never think to marry?

PIZARRO. With my parentage? The only women who would have had me weren't the sort you married. Spain's a pile of horsedung . . . When I began to think of a world here, something in me was longing for a new place like a country after rain, washed clear of all the badges and barriers, the pebbles men drop to tell them where they are

30

on a plain that's got no landmarks. I used to look after women with hope, but they didn't have much time for me. One of them said – what was it? – my soul was frostbitten. That's a word for you – Frostbitten. How goes it, man?

VASCA (*off*). A clear night, sir. Everything clear.

PIZARRO. I had a girl once, on a rock by the Southern Ocean. I lay with her one afternoon in winter, wrapped up in her against the cold, and the sea-fowl screaming, and it was the best hour of my life. I felt then that sea-water and bird droppings and the little pits in human flesh were all linked together for some great end right out of the net of words to catch. Not just my words, but anyone's. Then I lost it. Time came back. For always.

He moves away, feeling his side.

DE SOTO. Does it pain you?

PIZARRO. Oh, yes: *that's* still fierce.

DE SOTO. You should try to sleep. We'll need our strength.

PIZARRO. Listen, listen! Everything we feel is made of Time. All the beauties of life are shaped by it. Imagine a fixed sunset: the last note of a song that hung an hour, or a kiss for half of it. Try and halt a moment in our lives and it becomes maggoty at once. Even that word 'moment' is wrong, since that would mean a speck of time, something you could pick up on a rag and peer at . . . But that's the awful trap of life. You can't escape maggots unless you go with Time, and if you go, they wriggle in you anyway.

DE SOTO. This is gloomy talk.

YOUNG MARTIN *groans in his sleep.*

PIZARRO. For a gloomy time. You were talking women. I loved them with all the juice in me – but oh, the cheat in that tenderness. What is it but a lust to own their beauty, not them, which you never can: like trying to own the beauty of a goblet by paying for it. And even if you could it would become you and get soiled . . . I'm an old man, Cavalier, I can explain nothing. What I mean is: Time whipped up the lust in me and Time purged it. I was dandled on Time's knee and made to gurgle, then put to my sleep. I've been cheated from the moment I was born because there's death in everything.

DE SOTO. Except in God.

A pause.

PIZARRO. When I was young, I used to sit on the slope outside the village and watch the sun go down, and I used to think: if only I could find the place where it sinks to rest for the night, I'd find the source of life, like the beginning of a river. I used to wonder what it could be like. Perhaps an island, a strange place of white sand, where the people never died. Never grew old, or felt pain, and never died.

DE SOTO. Sweet fancy.

PIZARRO. It's what your mind runs to when it lacks instruction. If I had a son, I'd kill him if he didn't read his book. . . . Where does the sun rest at night?

DE SOTO. Nowhere. It's a heavenly body sent by God to move round the earth in perpetual motion.

PIZARRO. Do you know this?

DE SOTO. All Europe knows it.

PIZARRO. What if they were wrong? If it settled here each evening, somewhere in those great mountains, like a God laid down to sleep? To a savage mind it must make a fine God. I myself can't fix anything nearer to a thought of worship than standing at dawn and watching it fill the world. Like the coming of something eternal, against going flesh. What a fantastic wonder that anyone on earth should dare to say: 'That's my father. My father: the sun!' It's silly – but tremendous . . . You know – strange nonsense: since first I heard of him I've dreamed of him every night. A black king with glowing eyes, sporting the sun for a crown. What does it mean?

DE SOTO. I've no skill with dreams. Perhaps a soothsayer would tell you: 'The Inca's your enemy. You dream his emblem to increase your hate.'

PIZARRO. But I feel no enemy.

DE SOTO. Surely you do.

PIZARRO. No. Only that of all meetings I have made in my

life, this with him is the one I have to make. Maybe it's my death. Or maybe new life. I feel just this: all my days have been a path to this one morning.

OLD MARTIN. The sixteenth of November 1532. First light, sir.

XI

Lights brighten slowly.

VALVERDE (*singing, off*). Exsurge Domine.

SOLDIERS (*singing in unison*). Exsurge Domine.
    All the company comes on, chanting.

VALVERDE. Deus meus eripe me de manu peccatoris.

SOLDIERS. Deus meus eripe me de manu peccatoris.
    All kneel, spread across the stage.

VALVERDE. Many strong bulls have compassed me.

DE NIZZA. They have gaped upon me with their mouths, as a lion ravening.

VALVERDE. I am poured out like water, and all my bones are scattered.

DE NIZZA. My heart is like wax, melting in the midst of my bowels. My tongue cleaves to my jaws, and thou hast brought me into the dust of death.
    All freeze.

OLD MARTIN. The dust of death. It was in our noses. The full scare came to us quickly, like plague.
    All heads turn.

The men were crammed in buildings all round the square.
    All stand.

They stood there shivering, making water where they stood. An hour went by. Two. Three.
    All remain absolutely still.

Five. Not a move from the Indian camp. Not a sound from us. Only the weight of the day. A hundred and sixty men in full armour, cavalry mounted, infantry at the ready, standing in dead silence – glued in a trance of waiting.

PIZARRO. Hold fast now. Come on – you're Gods. Take heart. Don't blink your eyes, that's too much noise.

OLD MARTIN. Seven.

PIZARRO. Stiff. Stiff. You're your own masters, boys. Not peasant anymore. This is your time. Own it. Live it.

OLD MARTIN. Nine. Ten hours passed. There were few of us then who didn't feel the cold begin to crawl.

PIZARRO (*whispering*). Send him, send him, send him, send him.

OLD MARTIN. Dread comes with the evening air. Even the priest's arm fails.

PIZARRO. The sun's going out!

OLD MARTIN. No one looks at his neighbour. Then, with the shadow of night already running towards us—

YOUNG MARTIN. *They're coming!* Look, down the hill—

DE SOTO. How many?

YOUNG MARTIN. Hundreds, sir.

DE CANDIA. Thousands – two or three.

PIZARRO. Can you see *him*?

DE CANDIA. No, not yet.

DOMINGO. What's that – out there in front – they're doing something.

VASCA. Looks like sweeping—

DIEGO. They're sweeping the road!

DOMINGO. For *him*! They're sweeping the road for him! Five hundred of 'em sweeping the road!

SALINAS. God in Heaven!

PIZARRO. Are they armed?

DE CANDIA. To the teeth!

DE SOTO. How?—

DE CANDIA. Axes and spears.

YOUNG MARTIN. They're all glittering, glittering red!—

DIEGO. It's the sun! Like someone's stabbed it!—

VASCA. Squirting blood all over the sky!

DOMINGO. It's an omen!—

SALINAS. Shut up.

DOMINGO. It must be. The whole country's bleeding. Look for yourself. It's an omen!

VALVERDE. This is the day foretold you by the Angel of the Apocalypse. Satan reigns on the altars, jeering at the true God. The earth teems with corrupt kings.

DOMINGO. Oh God! Oh God! Oh God! Oh God!

DE SOTO. Control yourself!

DE CANDIA. They're stopping!

YOUNG MARTIN. They're throwing things down, sir!

PIZARRO. What things?

DE CANDIA. Weapons.

PIZARRO. No!

DIEGO. Yes, sir. I can see. All their weapons. They're throwing them down in a pile.

VASCA. They're laying down their arms.

SALINAS. I don't believe it!

VASCA. They are. They are leaving everything!

DOMINGO. It's a miracle.

DE SOTO. Why? *Why?*

PIZARRO. Because we're Gods. You see? You don't approach Gods with weapons.

Strange music faintly in the distance. Through all the ensuing it grows louder and louder.

DE SOTO. What's that?

YOUNG MARTIN. It's *him*. He's coming, sir.

PIZARRO. Where?

YOUNG MARTIN. *There*, sir.

DIEGO. Oh, look, *look*. God Almighty, it's not happening! . . .

DE SOTO. Steady man.

PIZARRO. You're coming. Come on then! *Come on!*

DE SOTO. General, it's time to hide.

PIZARRO. Yes, quick now. No one must be seen but the priests. Out there in the middle, Fathers: everyone else in hiding.

DE SOTO. Quick! jump to it!

Only now do the men break, scatter and vanish.

PIZARRO (*to* YOUNG MARTIN). You too.

YOUNG MARTIN. Until the fighting, sir?

PIZARRO. All the time for you, fighting or no.

YOUNG MARTIN. Oh no, sir!

35

PIZARRO. Do as I say. Take him, de Soto.

DE SOTO. Save you, General.

PIZARRO. And you, de Soto. San Jago!

DE SOTO. San Jago! Come on.

DE CANDIA. There are seven gunners on the roof. And three over there.

PIZARRO. Watch the cross-fire.

DE CANDIA. I'll wait for your signal.

PIZARRO. Then sound yours.

DE CANDIA. You'll hear it.

PIZARRO (*to* FELIPILLO). Felipillo! Stand there! Now . . . now . . . NOW!

He hurries off.

XII

The music crashes over the stage as the Indian procession enters in an astonishing explosion of colour. The King's attendants – many of them playing musical instruments: reed pipes, cymbals, and giant marraccas – are as gay as parrots. They wear costumes of orange and yellow, and fantastic head-dresses of gold and feathers, with eyes embossed on them in staring black enamel. By contrast, ATAHUALLPA INCA *presents a picture of utter simplicity. He is dressed from head to foot in white: across his eyes is a mask of jade mosaic, and round his head a circlet of plain gold. Silence falls. The King glares about him.*

ATAHUALLPA (*haughtily*). Where is the God?

VALVERDE (*through* FELIPILLO). I am a Priest of God.

ATAHUALLPA. I do not want the priest. I want the God. Where is he? He sent me greeting.

VALVERDE. That was our General. Our God cannot be seen.

ATAHUALLPA. *I* may see him.

VALVERDE. No. He was killed by men and went into the sky.

ATAHUALLPA. A God cannot be killed. See my father. You cannot kill him. He lives for ever and looks over his children every day.

VALVERDE. I am the answer to all mysteries. Hark, pagan and I will expound.

OLD MARTIN. And so he did, from the Creation to Our Lord's ascension.

He goes off.

VALVERDE (*walking among the Indians to the right*). And when he went he left the Pope as Regent for him.

DE NIZZA (*walking among the Indians to the left*). And when he went he left the Pope as Regent for him.

VALVERDE. He has commanded our King to bring all men to belief in the true God.

VALVERDE
DE NIZZA (*together*) } In Christ's name therefore I charge you: yield yourself his willing vassal.

ATAHUALLPA. I am the vassal of no man. I am the greatest Prince on earth. Your King is great. He has sent you far across the water. So he is my brother. But your Pope is mad. He gives away countries that are not his. His faith also is mad.

VALVERDE. Beware!

ATAHUALLPA. Ware you! You kill my people; you make them slaves. By what power?

VALVERDE. By this. (*He offers a Bible*) The Word of God.

ATAHUALLPA *holds it to his ear. He listens intently. He shakes it.*

ATAHUALLPA. No word.

He smells the book, and then licks it. Finally he throws it down impatiently.

God is angry with your insults.

VALVERDE. Blasphemy!

ATAHUALLPA. God is angry.

VALVERDE. Francisco Pizarro, do you stay your hand when Christ is insulted? Let this pagan feel the power of your arm. I absolve you all! San Jago!

37

PIZARRO *appears above with drawn sword, and in a great voice sings out his battle-cry:*

PIZARRO. SAN JAGO Y CIERRA ESPAÑA!

Instantly from all sides the soldiers rush in, echoing the great cry.

SOLDIERS. SAN JAGO!

There is a tense pause. The Indians look at this ring of armed men in terror. A violent drumming begins, and there ensues:

THE MIME OF THE GREAT MASSACRE

To a savage music, wave upon wave of Indians are slaughtered and rise again to protect their lord who stands bewildered in their midst. It is all in vain. Relentlessly the Spanish soldiers hew their way through the ranks of feathered attendants towards their quarry. They surround him. SALINAS *snatches the crown off his head and tosses it up to* PIZARRO, *who catches it and to a great shout crowns himself. All the Indians cry out in horror. The drum hammers on relentlessly while* ATAHUALLPA *is led off at sword-point by the whole band of Spaniards. At the same time, dragged from the middle of the sun by howling Indians, a vast bloodstained cloth bellies out over the stage. All rush off; their screams fill the theatre. The lights fade out slowly on the rippling cloth of blood.*

Act Two

THE KILL

I

Darkness. A bitter Inca lament is intoned, above.

Lights up a little. The bloodstained cloth still lies over the stage. In the sun chamber ATAHUALLPA *stands in chains, his back to the audience, his white robe dirty with blood. Although he is unmasked, we cannot yet see his face, only a tail of black hair hanging down his neck.*

OLD MARTIN *appears. From opposite,* YOUNG MARTIN *comes in, stumbling with shock. He collapses on his knees.*

OLD MARTIN. Look at the warrior where he struts. Glory on his sword. Salvation in his new spurs. One of the knights at last. The very perfect knight Sir Martin, tender in virtue, bodyguard of Christ Jesus, we are all eased out of kids' dreams; but who can be ripped out of them and live loving after? Three thousand Indians we killed in that square. The only Spaniard to be wounded was the General, scratched by a sword whilst protecting his Royal prisoner. That night, as I knelt vomiting into a canal, the empire of the Incas stopped. The spring of the clock was snapped. For a thousand miles men sat down not knowing what to do.

Enter DE SOTO.

DE SOTO. Well, boy, what is it? They weren't armed, is that it? If they had been we could be dead now.

YOUNG MARTIN. Honourably dead! Not alive and shamed.

DE SOTO. And Christ would be dead here too, scarcely born. When I first breathed blood it was in my lungs for days. But the time comes when you won't even sniff when it pours over your feet. See, boy, here and now it's kill or get killed. And if we go, we betray Christ, whose coming we are here to make.

39

YOUNG MARTIN. You talk as if we're butlers, sent to open the door for him.

DE SOTO. So we are.

YOUNG MARTIN. No! He's with us now – at all times – or never.

DE SOTO. He's with us, yes, but not with them. After he is, there will be time for mercy.

YOUNG MARTIN. When there is no danger! Some mercy!

DE SOTO. Would you put Christ in danger, then?

YOUNG MARTIN. He can look after himself.

DE SOTO. He can't. That's why he needs servants.

YOUNG MARTIN. To kill for him?

DE SOTO. If necessary. And it was. My parish priest used to say: There must always be dying to make new life. I think of that whenever I draw the sword. My constant thought is: I must be winter for Our Lord to be Spring.

YOUNG MARTIN. I don't understand.

    PIZARRO *and* FELIPILLO *come in.*

PIZARRO. Stand up when the Second addresses you. What are you, a defiled girl? (*To* DE SOTO) I've sent de Candia back to the Garrison. Reinforcements should be there presently. Come now: let's meet this King.

II

Lights up more.

They move upstage and bow. Above, OELLO *and* INTI COUSSI *come in and kneel on either side of the Inca, who ignores the embassy below.*

My lord, I am Francisco Pizarro, General of Spain. It is an honour to speak with you. (*Pause*) You are very tall, my lord. In my country are no such tall men. (*Pause*) My lord, won't you speak?

    ATAHUALLPA *turns. For the first time we see his face, carved in a mould of serene arrogance. His whole bearing displays the most entire dignity and natural grace. When he moves or speaks, it is always with the consciousness of his divine origin, his sacred function and his absolute power.*

ATAHUALLPA (*to* FELIPILLO). Tell him I am Atahuallpa Capac, Son of the Sun, Sun of the Moon, Lord of the Four Quarters. Why does he not kneel?

FELIPILLO. The Inca says he wishes he had killed you when you first came.

PIZARRO. Why didn't he?

ATAHUALLPA. He lied to me. He is not a God. I came for blessing. He sharpened his knives on the shoulders of my servants. I have no word for *him* whose word is evil.

FELIPILLO. He says he wants to make slaves of your best warriors, then kill all the others. Especially you he would kill because you are old; no use as slave.

PIZARRO. Tell him he will live to rue those intentions.

FELIPILLO. You make my master angry. He will kill you tomorrow. Then he will give that wife (*he indicates* OELLO) to me for my pleasure.

OELLO *rises in alarm.*

ATAHUALLPA. How dare you speak this before my face?

YOUNG MARTIN. General.

PIZARRO. What?

YOUNG MARTIN. Excuse me, sir, but I don't think you're being translated aright.

PIZARRO. You don't?

YOUNG MARTIN. No sir. Nor the King to you. I know a little of the language and he said nothing about slaves.

PIZARRO. You! What are you saying?

FELIPILLO. General Lord. This boy know nothing how to speak.

YOUNG MARTIN. I know more than you think. I know you're lying . . . He's after the woman, General. I saw him before, in the square, grabbing at her.

PIZARRO. Is that true?

YOUNG MARTIN. As I live, sir.

PIZARRO. What do you say?

41

The Royal Hunt of the Sun

FELIPILLO. General Lord, I speak wonderful for you. No one speak so wonderful.

PIZARRO. What about that girl?

FELIPILLO. You give her as present to me, yes?

PIZARRO. The Inca's wife?

FELIPILLO. Inca has many wives. This one small, not famous.

PIZARRO. Get out.

FELIPILLO. General Lord!

PIZARRO. You work another trick like this and I'll swear I'll hang you. Out!

FELIPILLO *spits at him and runs off.*

PIZARRO. Could you take his place?

YOUNG MARTIN. With work, sir.

PIZARRO. Work, then. Come, let's make a start. Ask him his age.

YOUNG MARTIN. My lord, (*hesitantly*) how old are him? I mean 'you' . . .

ATAHUALLPA. I have been on earth thirty and three years. What age is your master?

YOUNG MARTIN. Sixty-three.

ATAHUALLPA. All those years have taught him nothing but wickedness.

YOUNG MARTIN. That's not true.

PIZARRO. What does he say?

YOUNG MARTIN. I don't quite understand, my lord . . .

Exit YOUNG MARTIN.

OLD MARTIN. So it was I became the General's interpreter and was privy to everything that passed between them during the next months. The Inca tongue was very hard, but to please my adored master I worked at it for hours, and with each passing day found out more of it.

PIZARRO *leaves, followed by* DE SOTO.

42

III

Re-enter YOUNG MARTIN *above*. OLD MARTIN *watches below before going off.*

YOUNG MARTIN. Good day, my lord. I have a game here to amuse you. No Spaniard is complete without them. I take half and you take half. Then we fight. These are the Churchmen with their pyxes. The Nobility with their swords. The Merchants with their gold, and the Poor with their sticks.

ATAHUALLPA. What are the poor?

YOUNG MARTIN. Those who've got no gold. They suffer for this.

ATAHUALLPA (*crying out*). Aiyah!

YOUNG MARTIN. What are you thinking, my lord?

ATAHUALLPA. That my people will suffer.

    Enter PIZARRO *and* DE SOTO.

PIZARRO. Good day, my lord. How are you this morning?

ATAHUALLPA. You want gold. That is why you came here.

PIZARRO. My lord—

ATAHUALLPA. You can't hide from me. (*Showing him the card of the Poor*) You want gold. I know. Speak.

PIZARRO. You have gold?

ATAHUALLPA. It is the sweat of the sun. It belongs to me.

PIZARRO. Is there much?

ATAHUALLPA. Make me free. I would fill this room.

PIZARRO. Fill?

DE SOTO. It's not possible.

ATAHUALLPA. I am Atahuallpa and I say it.

PIZARRO. How long?

ATAHUALLPA. Two showings of my Mother Moon. But it will not be done.

PIZARRO. Why not?

ATAHUALLPA. You must swear to free me and you have no swear to give.

PIZARRO. You wrong me, my lord.

E   43

ATAHUALLPA. No, it is in your face, no swear.

PIZARRO. I never broke word with you. I never promised you safety. If once I did, you would have it.

ATAHUALLPA. Do you now?

DE SOTO. Refuse, sir. You could never free him.

PIZARRO. It won't come to that.

DE SOTO. It could.

PIZARRO. Never. Can you think how much gold it would take? Even half would drown us in riches.

DE SOTO. General, you can only give your word where you can keep it.

PIZARRO. I'll never have to break it. It's the same case.

DE SOTO. It's not.

PIZARRO. Oh, God's wounds, your niceties! He's offering more than any conqueror has even seen. Alexander, Tamberlaine, or who you please. I mean to have it.

DE SOTO. So. At your age gold is no lodestone!

PIZARRO. No more is it. I promised my men gold. Yes? He stands between them and that gold. If I don't make this bargain now he'll die; the men will demand it.

DE SOTO. And what's that to you if he does?

PIZARRO. I want him alive. At least for a while.

DE SOTO. You're thinking of how you dreamed of him.

PIZARRO. Yes. He has some meaning for me, this Man-God. An immortal man in whom all his people live completely. He has an answer for time.

DE SOTO. If it was true.

PIZARRO. Yes, if . . .

DE SOTO. General, be careful. I don't understand you in full but I know this: what you do now can never be undone.

PIZARRO. Words, my dear Cavalier. They don't touch me. This way I'll have gold for my men and him there safe. That's enough for the moment. (*To* ATAHUALLPA) Now you must keep the peace meanwhile, not strive to escape, nor urge your men to help you. So swear.

ATAHUALLPA. I swear!

PIZARRO. Then I swear too. Fill that room with gold and I will set you free.

44

DE SOTO. General!

PIZARRO. Oh, come man! He never will.

DE SOTO. I think this man performs what he swears. Pray God we don't pay bitterly for this.

He goes off. Enter OLD MARTIN.

PIZARRO. My lord – (ATAHUALLPA *ignores him*) – well spoken, lad. Your services increase every day.

YOUNG MARTIN. Thank you, sir.

The General leaves the stage and the boy goes out of the Sun chamber, leaving ATAHUALLPA *alone in it.*

OLD MARTIN. The room was twenty-two feet long by seventeen feet wide. The mark on the wall was nine feet high.

The Inca adopts a pose of command. Drums mark each name.

ATAHUALLPA. Atahuallpa speaks! (*A crash of instruments*) Atahuallpa needs. (*Crash*) Atahuallpa commands. (*Crash*) Bring him gold. From the palaces. From the temples. From all buildings in the great places. From walls of pleasure and roofs of omen. From floors of feasting and ceilings of death. Bring him the gold of Quito and Pachamanac! Bring him the gold of Cuzco and Coricancha! Bring him the gold of Vilcanota! Bring him the gold of Colae! Of Aymaraes and Arequipa! Bring him the gold of the Chimu! Put up a mountain of gold and free your Sun from his prison of clouds.

Lights down above. ATAHUALLPA *leaves the chamber.*

OLD MARTIN. It was agreed that the gold collected was not to be melted beforehand into bars, so that the Inca got the benefit of the space between them. Then he was moved out of his prison to make way for the treasure and given more comfortable state.

IV

Lights fade above, and brighten below.

Slowly the great cloth of blood is dragged off by two Indians as ATAHUALLPA *appears. He advances to the middle of the stage. He claps his hands, once. Immediately a gentle hum is heard and Indians appear with new clothing. From their wrists hang tiny golden cymbals and small bells; to the soft clash and tinkle of these little instruments his servant removes the Inca's bloodstained garments and puts on him clean ones.*

OLD MARTIN. He was allowed to audience his nobles. The little loads they bore were a sign of reverence.

VILLAC UMU *and* CHALLCUCHIMA *come in.*

He was dressed in his royal cloak, made from the skins of vampire birds, and his ears were hung again with the weight of noble responsibility.

ATAHUALLPA *is cloaked, a collar of turquoises is placed round his neck and heavy gold rings are placed in his ears. While this is happening there is a fresh tinkling and more Indians appear, carrying his meal in musical dishes – plates like tambourines from whose rims hang bells, or in whose lower shelves are tiny golden balls. The stage is filled with chimes and delicate clatter, and above it the perpetual humming of masked servants.*

OLD MARTIN. His meals are served as they always had been. I remember his favourite food was stewed lamb, garnished with sweet potatoes.

The food is served to the Inca in this manner. OELLO *takes meat out of a bowl, places it in her hands and* ATAHUALLPA *lowers his face to it, while she turns her own face away from him out of respect.*

OLD MARTIN. What he didn't eat was burnt, and if he spilled any on himself, his clothes were burnt also. (*Exit*)

OELLO *rises and quietly removes the dish. Suddenly*

46

FELIPILLO *rushes on and knocks it violently from her hand.*

FELIPILLO. You're going to burn it? Why? Because your husband is a God? How stupid! stupid! stupid!

He grabs her and flings her to the ground. A general cry of horror.

(*To* ATAHUALLPA) Yes, I touch her! Make me dead! You are a God. Make me dead with your eyes!

VILLAC UMU. What you have said kills you. You will be buried in the earth alive.

A pause. For a moment FELIPILLO *half believes this. Then he laughs and kisses the girl on the throat. As she screams and struggles,* YOUNG MARTIN *rushes in.*

YOUNG MARTIN. Felipillo, stop it!

VALVERDE *comes in from another side, with* DE NIZZA.

VALVERDE. Felipillo! Is it for this we saved you from Hell? Your old God encouraged lust. Your new God will damn you for it. Leave him!

FELIPILLO *runs off.*

(*To the* INDIANS) Go!

A pause. No one moves until ATAHUALLPA *claps his hands twice. Then all the servants bow and leave.*

Now, my lord, let us take up our talk again. Tell me – I am only a simple priest – as an undoubted God, do you live forever here on earth?

VILLAC UMU. Here on earth Gods come one after another, young and young again, to protect the people of the Sun. Then they go up to his great place in the sky, at his will.

VALVERDE. What if they are killed in battle?

VILLAC UMU. If it is not the Sun's time for them to go, he will return them to life again in the next day's light.

VALVERDE. How comforting. And has any Inca so returned?

VILLAC UMU. No.

VALVERDE. Curious.

VILLAC UMU. This means only that all Incas have died in the Sun's time.

VALVERDE. Clever.

VILAC UMU. No. True.

VALVERDE. Tell me this, how can the Sun have a child?

VILLAC UMU. How can your God have a Child, since you say he has no body?

VALVERDE. He is a spirit – inside us.

VILLAC UMU. Your God is inside you? How can this be?

ATAHUALLPA. They eat him. First he becomes a biscuit, and then they eat him. (*The Inca bares his teeth and laughs soundlessly*) I have seen this. At praying they say 'This is the body of our God'. Then they drink his blood. It is very bad. Here in my empire we do not eat men. My family forbade it many years past.

VALVERDE. You are being deliberately stupid.

VILLAC UMU. Why do you eat your God? To have his strength?

DE NIZZA. Yes, my lord.

VILLAC UMU. But your God is weak. He fights with no man. That is why he was killed.

DE NIZZA. He wanted to be killed, so he could share death with us.

ATAHUALLPA. So he needed killers to help him, though you say killing is bad.

VALVERDE. This is the devil's tongue.

DE NIZZA. My lord must see that when God becomes man, he can no longer act perfectly.

ATAHUALLPA. Why?

DE NIZZA. He joins us in the prison of our sin.

ATAHUALLPA. What is sin?

DE NIZZA. Let me picture it to you as a prison cell, the bars made of our imperfections. Through them we glimpse a fair country where it is always morning. We wish we could walk there, or else forget the place entirely. But we cannot snap the bars, or if we do, others grow in their stead.

ATAHUALLPA. All your pictures are of prisons and chains.

DE NIZZA. All life is chains. We are chained to food, and

fire in the winter. To innocence lost but its memory unlost. And to needing each other.

ATAHUALLPA. I need no one.

DE NIZZA. That is not true.

ATAHUALLPA. I am the Sun. I need only the sky.

DE NIZZA. That is not true, Atahuallpa. The sun is a ball of fire. Nothing more.

ATAHUALLPA. How?

DE NIZZA. Nothing more.

With terrible speed, the INCA *rises to strike* DE NIZZA.

VALVERDE. Down! Do you dare lift your hand against a priest? Sit! Now!

ATAHUALLPA *does not move.*

DE NIZZA. You do not feel your people, my lord, because you do not love them.

ATAHUALLPA. Explain love.

DE NIZZA. It is not known in your kingdom. At home we can say to our ladies: 'I love you', or to our native earth. It means we rejoice in their lives. But a man cannot say this to the woman he must marry at twenty-five; or to the strip of land allotted to him at birth which he must till until he dies. Love must be free, or else it alters away. Command it to your court: it will send a deputy. Let God order it to fill our hearts, it becomes useless to him. It is stronger than iron: yet in a fist or force it melts. It is a coin that sparkles in the hand: yet in the pocket it turns to rust. Love is the only door from the prison of ourselves. It is the eagerness of God to enter that prison, to take on pain, and imagine lust, so that the torn soldier, or the spent lecher, can call out in his defeat: 'You know this too, so help me from it.'

A further music of bells and humming. Enter OLD MARTIN.

THE FIRST GOLD PROCESSION

Guarded closely by Spanish soldiers, a line of Indian porters comes in, each carrying a stylized gold object

49

– utensils and ornaments. They cross the stage and disappear. Almost simultaneously, above, similar objects are hung up by Indians in the middle of the sun.

OLD MARTIN (*during this*). The first gold arrived. Much of it was in big plates weighing up to seventy-five pounds, the rest in objects of amazing skill. Knives of ceremony; collars and fretted crowns; funeral gloves, and red-stained death masks, goggling at us with profound enamel eyes. Some days there were things worth thirty or forty gold pesos – but we weren't satisfied with that. (*Exit*).

Enter PIZARRO *and* DE SOTO.

PIZARRO. I find you wanting in honesty. A month has passed: the room isn't a quarter full.

ATAHUALLPA. My kingdom is great; porters are slow. You will see more gold before long.

PIZARRO. The rumour is we'll see a rising before long.

ATAHUALLPA. Not a leaf stirs in my kingdom without my leave. If you do not trust me send to Cuzco, my capital. See how quiet my people sit.

PIZARRO (*to* DE SOTO). Good. You leave immediately with a force of thirty.

CHALCUCHIMA. God is tied by his word, like you. But if he raise one nail of one finger of one hand, you would all die that same raising.

PIZARRO. So be it. If you play us false, both these will die before us.

ATAHUALLPA. There are many Priests, many Generals. These can die.

VALVERDE. Mother of God! There's no conversion possible for this man.

DE SOTO. You cannot say that, sir.

VALVERDE. Satan has many forms and there sits one. As for his advisers, it is you, Priest, who stiffen him against me. You, General, who whisper revolt.

CHALCUCHIMA. You lie.

VALVERDE. Leave him!

As before they do not move until ATAHUALLPA

has clapped his hands twice. Then, immediately, the two Indians bow and leave.

Pagan filth.

DE SOTO. I'll make inspection. Good-bye my lord, we'll meet in a month.

Exit DE SOTO.

VALVERDE. Beware Pizarro. Give him the slack, he will destroy us all.

He goes out another way.

DE NIZZA. The Father has great zeal.

PIZARRO. Oh, yes, great zeal to see the devil in a poor dark man.

DE NIZZA. Not so poor, General. A man who is the soul of his kingdom. Look hard, you *will* find Satan here, because here is a country which denies the right to hunger.

PIZARRO. You call hunger a right?

DE NIZZA. Of course, it gives life meaning. Look around you: happiness has no feel for men here since they are forbidden unhappiness. They have everything in common so they have nothing to give each other. They are part of the seasons, no more; as indistinguishable as mules, as predictable as trees. All men are born unequal: this is a divine gift. And want is their birthright. Where you deny this and there is no hope of any new love; where tomorrow is abolished, and no man ever thinks 'I can change myself', there you have the rule of Anti-Christ. Atahuallpa, I will not rest until I have brought you to the true God.

ATAHUALLPA. No! He is not true! Where is he? There is my father-Sun! You see now only by his wish; yet try to see into him and he will darken your eyes for ever. With hot burning he pulls the corn and we feed. With cold burning he shrinks it and we starve. These are his burnings and our life. Do not speak to me again of your God: he is nowhere.

PIZARRO *laughs. Hurriedly* DE NIZZA *leaves.*

51

V

PIZARRO. You said you'd hear the Holy Men.

ATAHUALLPA. They are fools.

PIZARRO. They are not fools.

ATAHUALLPA. Do you believe them?

PIZARRO. For certain.

ATAHUALLPA. Look into me.

PIZARRO. Your eyes are smoking wood.

ATAHUALLPA. You do not believe them.

PIZARRO. You dare not say that to me . . .

ATAHUALLPA. You do not believe them. Their God is not in your face.

> PIZARRO *retreats from* ATAHUALLPA, *who begins to sing in a strange voice:*

> You must not rob, O little finch.
> The harvest maize, O little finch.
> The trap is set, O little finch.
> To seize you quick, O little finch.

> Ask that black bird, O little finch.
> Nailed on a branch, O little finch.
> Where is her heart, O little finch.
> Where are her plumes, O little finch.

> She is cut up, O little finch.
> For stealing grain, O little finch.
> See, see the fate, O little finch.
> Of robber birds, O little finch.

This is a harvest song. For you.

PIZARRO. For me?

ATAHUALLPA. Yes.

PIZARRO. Robber birds.

ATAHUALLPA. Yes.

PIZARRO. You're a robber bird yourself.

ATAHUALLPA. Explain this.

PIZARRO. You killed your brother to get the throne.

ATAHUALLPA. He was a fool. His body was a man. His head was a child.

PIZARRO. But he was the rightful king.

ATAHUALLPA. I was the rightful God. My Sky Father shouted 'Rise up! In you lives your Earth Father, Huayana the Warrior. Your brother is fit only to tend herds but you were born to tend my people.' So I killed him, and the land smiled.

PIZARRO. That was my work long ago. Tending herds.

ATAHUALLPA. It was not your work. You are a warrior. It is in your face.

PIZARRO. You see much in my face.

ATAHUALLPA. I see your father.

PIZARRO. You do me honour, lad.

ATAHUALLPA. Speak true. If in your home your brother was King, but fit only for herds, would you take his crown?

PIZARRO. If I could.

ATAHUALLPA. And then you would kill him.

PIZARRO. No.

ATAHUALLPA. If you could not keep it for fear of his friends, unless he was dead, you would kill him.

PIZARRO. Let me give you another case. If I come to a country and seize the King's crown, but for fear of his friends cannot keep it unless I kill him, what do I do?

ATAHUALLPA. So.

PIZARRO. So.

ATAHUALLPA *moves away, offended.*

Oh, it is only a game we play. Tell me – did you hate your brother?

ATAHUALLPA. No. He was ugly like a llama, like his mother. My mother was beautiful.

PIZARRO. I did not know my mother. She was not my father's wife. She left me at the church door for anyone to find. There's talk in the village still, how I was suckled by a sow.

ATAHUALLPA. You are not then . . . ?

PIZARRO. Legitimate? No, my lord, no more than you.

ATAHUALLPA. So.

PIZARRO. So.

A pause.

ATAHUALLPA. To be born so is a sign for a great man.

PIZARRO (*smiling*). I think so too.

> ATAHUALLPA *removes one of his golden earrings and hangs it on* PIZARRO'S *ear.*

And what is that?

ATAHUALLPA. The sign of a nobleman. Only the most important men may wear them, The most near to me.

YOUNG MARTIN. Very becoming, sir. Look.

> *He hands him a dagger. The General looks at himself in the blade.*

PIZARRO. I have never seemed so distinguished to myself. I thank you.

ATAHUALLPA. Now you must learn the dance of the aylu.

YOUNG MARTIN. The dance of a nobleman, sir.

ATAHUALLPA. Only he can do this. I will show you.

> PIZARRO *sits.* ATAHUALLPA *dances a ferocious mime of a warrior killing his foes. It is very difficult to execute, demanding great litheness and physical stamina. As suddenly as it began, it is over.*

ATAHUALLPA. You dance.

PIZARRO. I can't dance, lad.

ATAHUALLPA (*sternly*). You dance.

> *He sits to watch. Seeing there is no help for it,* PIZARRO *rises and clumsily tries to copy the dance. The effect is so grotesque that* YOUNG MARTIN *cannot help laughing. The General tries again, lunges, slips, slides, and finally starts to laugh himself. He gives up the attempt.*

PIZARRO (*to* ATAHUALLPA). You make me laugh! (*In sudden wonder.*) *You make me laugh!*

> ATAHUALLPA *consults his young interpreter, who tries to explain. The Inca nods gravely. Tentatively* PIZARRO *extends his hand to him.* ATAHUALLPA *takes it and rises. Quietly they go off together.*

VI

Enter OLD MARTIN.

OLD MARTIN. Slowly the pile increased. The army waited nervously and licked its lips. Greed began to rise in us like a tide of sea.

A music of bells and humming.

THE SECOND GOLD PROCESSION
and THE RAPE OF THE SUN.

Another line of Indian porters comes in, bearing gold objects. Like the first, this instalment of treasure is guarded by Spanish soldiers, but they are less disciplined now. Two of them assault an Indian and grab his headdress. Another snatches a necklace at sword's point.

Above, in the chamber, the treasure is piled up as before. DIEGO *and the* CHAVEZ *brothers are seen supervising. They begin to explore the sun itself, leaning out of the chamber and prodding at the petals with their halberds. Suddenly* DIEGO *gives a cry of triumph, drives his halberd into a slot in one of the rays, and pulls out the gold inlay. The sun gives a deep groan, like the sound of a great animal being wounded. With greedy yelps, all the soldiers below rush at the sun and start pulling it to bits; they tear out the gold inlays and fling them on the ground, while terrible groans fill the air. In a moment only the great gold frame remains; a broken, blackened sun.*

Enter DE SOTO.

DIEGO. Welcome back, sir.

DE SOTO. Diego, it's good to see you.

DIEGO. What's it like, sir? Is there trouble?

DE SOTO. It's grave quiet. Terrible. Men just standing in

55

fields for hundreds of miles. Waiting for their God to come back to them.

DIEGO. Well, if he does they'll be fighters again and we're for the limepit.

DE SOTO. How's the General?

DIEGO. An altered man. No one's ever seen him so easy. He spends hours each day with the King. He's going to find it hard when he has to do it.

DE SOTO. Do what?

DIEGO. Kill him, sir.

DE SOTO. He can't do that. Not after a contract witnessed before a whole army.

DIEGO. Well, he can't let him go, that's for certain . . . Never mind, he'll find a way. He's as cunning as the devil's gran-dad, save your pardon, sir.

DE SOTO. No, you're right, boy.

DIEGO. Tell us about their capital, then. What's it like?

During the preceding, a line of Indians, bent double, has been loaded with the torn-off petals from the sun. Now, as DE SOTO describes Cuzco, they file slowly round the stage and go off, staggering under the weight of the great gold slabs. When he reaches the account of the garden, the marvellous objects he tells of appear in the treasure chamber above, borne by Indians, and are stacked up until they fill it completely. The interior of the sun is now a solid mass of gold.

DE SOTO. Completely round. They call it the navel of the earth and that's what it looks like. In the middle was a huge temple, the centre of their faith. The walls were plated with gold, enough to blind us. Inside, set out on tables, golden platters for the sun to dine off. Outside, the garden: acres of gold soil planted with gold maize. Entire apple trees in gold. Gold birds on the branches. Gold geese and ducks. Gold butterflies in the air on silver strings. And – imagine this – away in a field, life-size, twenty golden llamas grazing with their kids. The garden of the Sun at Cuzco. A wonder of the earth. Look at it now.

DIEGO (*rushing in below*). Hey! The room's full!

DOMINGO. It isn't!

SALINAS. It is. Look!

JUAN. He's right. It's full!

DIEGO. We can start the share-out now. (*Cheers*)

PEDRO. What'll you do with your lot, Juan, boy?

JUAN. Buy a farm.

PEDRO. Me, too. I don't work for nobody ever again.

DOMINGO. Ah, you can buy a palace, easy, with a share of
that. Never mind a hissing farm! What d'you say,
Diego?

DIEGO. Oh, I want a farm, A good stud farm, and a stable
of Arabs, just for me to ride!

 Enter VASCA *rolling a huge gold sun, like a hoop.*

VASCA. Look what I got, boys! The sun! He ain't public
any more, the old sun. He's private property!

DOMINGO. There's no private property, till share out.

VASCA. Well, here's the exception. I risked my life to get this
a hundred feet up.

JUAN. Dungballs!

VASCA. I did! Off the temple roof.

PEDRO. Come on, boy, get it up there with the rest.

VASCA. No. Finding's keepings. That's the law.

JUAN. What law?

VASCA. My law. Do you think you'll see any of this once the
share-out starts? Not on your hissing life. You leave it up
there, boy, you won't see nothing again.

PEDRO (*to his brother*). He's right there.

JUAN. Do you think so?

VASCA. Of course. Officers first, then the Church. You'll get
hissing nothing. (*A pause*)

SALINAS. So let's have a share-out now, then!

DOMINGO. Why not? We're all entitled.

VASCA. Of course we are.

JUAN. All right. I'm with you.

PEDRO. Good boy!

SALINAS. Come on, then.

 They all make a rush for the Sun Chamber.

DE SOTO. Where do you think you're going? . . . You know the General's orders. Nothing till share-out. Penalty for breach, death. Disperse now. I'll go and see the General.

They hesitate.

(*Quietly*) Get to your posts.

Reluctantly, they disperse.

And keep a sharp watch. The danger's not over yet.

DIEGO. I'd say it had only just begun, sir.

He goes. DE SOTO *remains.*

VII

Enter PIZARRO *and* ATAHUALLPA *duelling furiously;* YOUNG MARTIN *behind. The Inca is a magnificent fighter and launches himself vigorously on the old man, finally knocking the sword from his hand.*

PIZARRO. Enough! You exhaust me . . .

ATAHUALLPA. I fight well – 'ye-es'?

From the difficulty he has with this word, it is evident that it is in Spanish.

PIZARRO (*imitating him*). 'Ye-es'! . . . Like a hidalgo!

YOUNG MARTIN. Magnificent, my lord.

PIZARRO. I'm proud of you.

ATAHUALLPA. Chica!

YOUNG MARTIN. Maize wine, sir.

PIZARRO. De Soto! – A drink, my dear second.

DE SOTO. With pleasure, General, the room is full.

PIZARRO (*casually*). I know it.

DE SOTO. My advice to you is to share out right away. The men are just on the turn.

PIZARRO. I think so too.

DE SOTO. We daren't delay.

PIZARRO. Agreed. Now I shall astound you, Cavalier. Atahuallpa, you have learnt how a Spaniard fights. Now you will learn his honour. Martin, your pen. (*Dictating*) 'Let this be known throughout my army. The Inca Atahuallpa has today discharged his obligation to General Pizarro. He is therefore a free man.'

DE SOTO (*toasting him*). My lord, your freedom!

ATAHUALLPA *kneels. Silently he mouths words of gratitude to the sun.*

ATAHUALLPA. Atahuallpa thanks the lord de Soto, the lord Pizarro, all lords of honour. You may touch my joy.

He extends his arms. Both Spaniards help to raise him.

DE SOTO. What happens now?

PIZARRO. I release him. He must swear first, of course, not to harm us.

DE SOTO. Do you think he will?

PIZARRO. For me he will.

ATAHUALLPA (*to the boy*). What is that you have done?

YOUNG MARTIN. Writing, my lord.

ATAHUALLPA. Explain this.

YOUNG MARTIN. These are signs: This is 'Atahuallpa', and this is 'ransom'.

ATAHUALLPA. You put this sign, and he will see and know 'ransom'?

YOUNG MARTIN. Yes.

ATAHUALLPA. No.

YOUNG MARTIN. Yes, my lord. I'll do it again.

ATAHUALLPA. Here, on my nail. Do not say what you put.

YOUNG MARTIN *writes on his nail.*

YOUNG MARTIN. Now show it to Cavalier de Soto.

He does so. DE SOTO *reads and whispers the word to* ATAHUALLPA.

ATAHUALLPA (*to the boy*). What is put?

YOUNG MARTIN. God.

ATAHUALLPA (*amazed*). God! . . . (*He stares at his nail in fascination then bursts into delighted laughter, like a child.*) Show me again! Another sign!

The boy writes on another nail.

PIZARRO. Tell Salinas to take five hundred Indians and melt everything down.

F   59

The Royal Hunt of the Sun

DE SOTO. Everything?

PIZARRO. We can't transport it as it is.

DE SOTO. But there are objects of great beauty, sir. In all my service I've never seen treasure like this. Work subtler than anything in Italy.

PIZARRO. You're a tender man.

ATAHUALLPA (*extending his nail to* PIZARRO). What is put?

PIZARRO (*who of course cannot read*). Put?

ATAHUALLPA. Here.

PIZARRO. This is a foolish game.

YOUNG MARTIN. The General never learnt the skill, my lord. (*An embarrassed pause*) A soldier does not need it.
    ATAHUALLPA *stares at him.*

ATAHUALLPA. A King needs it. There is great power in these marks. You are the King in this room. You must teach us two. We will learn together – like brothers.

PIZARRO. You would stay with me here, to learn?
    Pause.

ATAHUALLPA. No. Tomorrow I will go.

PIZARRO. And then? What will you do then?

ATAHUALLPA. I will not hurt you.

PIZARRO. Or my army?

ATAHUALLPA. That I do not swear.

PIZARRO. You must.

ATAHUALLPA. You do not say this till now.

PIZARRO. Well, now I say it. Atahuallpa, you must swear to me that you will not hurt a man in my army if I let you go.

ATAHUALLPA. I will not swear this.

PIZARRO. For my sake.

ATAHUALLPA. Three thousand of my servants they killed in the square. Three thousand, without arms. I will avenge them.

PIZARRO. There is a way of mercy, Atahuallpa.

ATAHUALLPA. It is not my way. It is not your way.

PIZARRO. Well, show it to me, then.

ATAHUALLPA. Keep your swear first.

PIZARRO. That I cannot do.

60

Act Two – The Kill

ATAHUALLPA. Cannot?

PIZARRO. Not immediately ... you must see: you are many, we are few.

ATAHUALLPA. This is not important.

PIZARRO. To me it is.

ATAHUALLPA hisses with fury. He strides across the room and before PIZARRO's face makes a violent gesture with his hand between their two mouths.

ATAHUALLPA (*violently*). You gave a word!

PIZARRO. And will keep it. Only not now. Not today.

ATAHUALLPA. When?

PIZARRO. Soon.

ATAHUALLPA. When?

PIZARRO. Very soon.

ATAHUALLPA (*falling on his knees and beating the ground*). *When?*

PIZARRO. As soon as you promise not to hurt my army.

ATAHUALLPA (*with wild rage*). I will kill every man of them! I will make drums of their bodies! I will beat music on them at my great feasts!

PIZARRO (*provoked*). Boy – what have I put?

YOUNG MARTIN. 'He is therefore a free man.'

PIZARRO. Continue: 'But for the welfare of the country, he will remain for the moment as guest of the army.'

DE SOTO. What does that mean?

ATAHUALLPA. What does he say?

PIZARRO. Don't translate.

DE SOTO. So it's started. My warning was nothing to you.

PIZARRO. Well, gloat, gloat!

DE SOTO. I don't gloat.

ATAHUALLPA. What does he say?

PIZARRO. Nothing.

ATAHUALLPA. There is fear in his face!

PIZARRO. *Be quiet!* ... (*To* DE SOTO) I want all the gold in blocks. Leave nothing unmelted. Attend to it yourself, personally!

DE SOTO goes abruptly. OLD MARTIN *appears in the background.* PIZARRO *is trembling.*

61

PIZARRO (*to the page*). Well, what are you staring at, Little Lord Chivalry? Get out!

YOUNG MARTIN. He trusts you, sir.

PIZARRO. Trust: what's that? Another word. Honour . . . glory . . . trust: your word – Gods!

YOUNG MARTIN. You can see it, sir. He trusts you.

PIZARRO. I told you: out.

YOUNG MARTIN (*greatly daring*). You can't betray him, sir. You can't.

PIZARRO. Damn you – impertinence!

YOUNG MARTIN. I don't care, sir. You just can't! (*He stops*)

PIZARRO. In all your study of those admirable writers, you never learned the duty a page owes his master. I am sorry you have not better fulfilled your first office. There will be no other.

> *The boy makes to go out.*

A salute, if you please.

> *He bows.*

Time was when we couldn't stop you.

> YOUNG MARTIN *leaves.* PIZARRO *stares after him, shaking.*

OLD MARTIN. I went out into the night – the cold high night of the Andes, hung with stars like crystal apples – and dropped my first tears as a man. My first and last. That was my first and last worship too. Devotion never came again. (*Exit*)

> *With a moan,* PIZARRO *collapses on the floor and lies writhing in pain.* ATAHUALLPA *contemplates his captor with surprised disdain. But slowly, as the old man's agony continues, contempt in the King is replaced by a gentler emotion. Curious, he kneels. Uncertain what to do, he extends his hands, first to the wound, and then to* PIZARRO's *head, which he holds with a kind of remote tenderness. The lights go down all around them.*

PIZARRO. Leave it now. There's no cure or more easing for it. Death's entered the house you see. It's half down already, like an old barn. What can you know about that? Youth's

Act Two – The Kill

in you like a spring of blood, to spurt for ever. Your skin is singing: 'I will never get old.' But you will. Time is stalking you, as I did. That gold flesh will cold and blacken. Your eyes will curdle, those wet living eyes . . . They'll make a mummy of your body – I know the custom – and wrap you in robes of vicuna wool, and carry you through all your Empire down to Cuzco. And then they'll fold you in two and sit you on a chair in darkness . . . Atahuallpa, I'm going to die! And the thought of that dark has for years rotted everything for me, all simple joy in life. All through old age, which is so much longer and more terrible than anything in youth, I've watched the circles of nature with hatred. The leaves pop out, the leaves fall. Every year it's piglet time, calving time, time for children in a gush of blood and water. Women dote on this. A birth, any birth, fills them with love. They clap with love, and my soul shrugs. Round and round is all I see: an endless sky of birds, flying and ripping and nursing their young to fly and rip and nurse their young – *for what*? Listen, boy. That prison the Priest calls Sin Original, I know as Time. And seen in time everything is trivial. Pain. Good. God is trivial in that seeing. Trapped in this cage we cry out 'There's a gaoler; there must be. At the last, last, last of lasts he will let us out. He will! He will!' . . . But, oh my boy, no one will come out for all our crying. (*Pause*) I'm going to kill you, Atahuallpa. What does it matter? Words kept, words broken, it all means nothing. Nothing. You go to sleep earlier than me, that's all. Do you see? Look at your eyes, like coals from the sun, glowing forever in the deep of your skull. Like my dream . . . Sing me your little song. (*Singing*.) O little finch. . . .

ATAHUALLPA *intones a few lines of the song.*

Nothing. Nothing . . . (*In sudden anguish, almost hatred*) O, lad, what am I going to do with you?

63

VIII

A red light up above.

OLD MARTIN *appears above in the Sun Chamber. Violent music, the sound of destruction. The light fades and comes up on stage where the soldiers assemble.*

OLD MARTIN. Nine forges were kept alight for three weeks. The masterwork of centuries was banged down into fat bars, four hundred and forty pounds each day. The booty exceeded all other known in history: the sack of Genoa, Milan or even Rome. Share-out started at once. (*Exit*)

DIEGO. General Francisco Pizarro, 57,220 gold pesos. Hernando de Soto, 17,740 gold pesos. The Holy Church, 2,220 gold pesos.

Enter ESTETE *and* DE CANDIA.

ESTETE. And a fifth of everything, of course, to the Crown.

PIZARRO. You come in good time, Veedor.

ESTETE. So it seems! Cavalier.

DE SOTO. Veedor.

PIZARRO. Welcome, de Candia.

DE CANDIA. Thank you. (*Indicating the ear-ring*) I see the living's become soft here already. The men hung with jewels like fops at Court.

PIZARRO. You set the fashion: I only follow.

DE CANDIA. I'm flattered.

PIZARRO. What news of the reinforcements?

DE CANDIA. None.

ESTETE. I sent runners back to the coast. They saw nothing.

PIZARRO. So we're cut off, here. How's my garrison?

DE CANDIA. Spanish justice reigns supreme. They hang Indians for everything. How's your royal friend? When do we hang him?

Pause. PIZARRO *tears off his ear-ring and flings it on the floor.*

PIZARRO. Finish the share-out.

Violently he leaves them. The men stare after him.

DE SOTO. Go on Diego. Tell us the rest . . . *Go on,* man!

DIEGO. The remainder – cavalry, infantry, clerks, farriers, coopers and the like – will divide a total of 971,000 gold pesos!

Cheers. Enter RODAS.

SALINAS. Well, look. Our little tailor! How are you, friend?

RODAS. Hungry. What do I get?

SALINAS. A kick up the tunnel.

RODAS. Ho, ha. Day of a hundred jokes! I got a right to a share.

DOMINGO. What for?

RODAS. I stayed behind and guarded your hissing rear, that's what for.

DE SOTO. You've no right, Rodas. As far as you cared we could all rot, remember? Well, now you get nothing; the proper wage for cowardice.

General agreement. The men settle upstage to a game of dice.

(*To* ESTETE) I must wait on the General.

ESTETE. I am sorry to see him still subject to distresses. I had hoped that victory would have brought him calmer temper.

DE CANDIA. It must be his new wealth, Veedor. So much, so sudden, must be a great burden to him.

DE SOTO. The burdens of the General, sir, are care for his men, and for our present situation. Let us try to lighten them for him as we can.

He goes off.

DE CANDIA. Let us indeed. One throat cut and we're all lightened.

ESTETE. It would much relieve the Crown if you'd cut it.

DE CANDIA. If I . . . ? You mean I'm not Spanish, I don't have to trouble with honour.

ESTETE. You're not a subject. It could be disowned by my King. And you have none.

DE CANDIA. So the Palace of Disinterest has a privy after all. Look man, you're the overseer here, so do your job. Go to the General and tell him the brownie must go. And

65

add this from me: if Spain waits any longer, Venice will act for herself.

They go off. Enter OLD MARTIN.

IX

A scene of tension and growing violence. The soldiers, now dirty almost beyond recognition, but wearing ornaments, earrings and headdresses stolen from the treasure, dice for gold. They are watched silently from above by a line of masked Indians carrying instruments for making bird noises. A drum begins to beat. PIZARRO *stumbles in, and during the whole ensuing scene limps to and fro across the stage like a caged animal, ignoring everything but his own mental pain.*

OLD MARTIN. Morale began to go fast. Day after day we watched his private struggle, and the brownies watched us, waiting one sign from the frozen boy to get up and kill the lot of us.

DOMINGO. Play up, then!

PEDRO. Two fours.

    JUAN *throws successfully.*

JUAN (*grabbing a gold bar belonging to* PEDRO). That's mine, boy.

PEDRO. No – Juan!

JUAN. Give it. (*He snatches it*)

DOMINGO. They say there's an army gathering in the mountains. At least five thousand of them.

VASCA. I heard that too.

DOMINGO. Blas says there's some of them cannibals.

    Bird cries.

SALINAS. That's just stories. Hissing stupid stories. You don't want to listen to 'em.

RODAS. I'd like to see you when they tie you to the spit.

VASCO (*rolling the dice*). Turn up! Turn up! Turn up!

RODAS. Come on boys, cut me in.

VASCA. Hiss off! No stake, no play.

66

RODAS. Bloody bastards!

DOMINGO. They say it's led by the Inca's top general. The brownies are full of his name.

VASCA. What is it? Rumi ... Rumi ... ?

DOMINGO. That's it. Ruminagui, something like that.

The Indians above repeat the name in a low menacing chant: RU-MIN-Ã-GUI! *The soldiers look fearfully about them. The bird cries sound again.*

SALINAS. Come on, then, let's play.

VASCA. What for? The sun?

SALINAS. The sun!

VASCA. Turn up! Turn up! Turn up! Turn up! King and ten. Beat that!

SALINAS. Holy Mary, mother of Christ. Save my soul and bless my dice. (*He throws*) Two Kings ... I did it! I'm sorry, lads, but that's your sun gone.

VASCA. Go on, then. Let's see you pick it up.

SALINAS bends and tries to shift it. VASCA *laughs. The bird cries grow wilder.*

RODAS. He can't even lift it, but I can't play!

SALINAS. I'll settle for these.

He picks up three gold bars and walks off with them. RODAS trips him up and he goes sprawling.

Christ damn you, Rodas – that's the hissing last I take from you.

He springs at RODAS and clouts him with a gold bar. The tailor howls, picks up another, and a fight starts between them which soon becomes a violent free-for-all. The men shout; the birds scream; the General paces to and fro, ignoring everything. Finally DE SOTO rushes on just in time as SALINAS tries to strangle RODAS. He is followed by ESTETE and the two priests, who attend to the wounded.

DE SOTO. *Stop this!* ... Do you want to start it all off? *Silence. All the Indians rise, above. Uneasily the soldiers stare up at them.*

You – night watch. You, you go with him. You take the East Gate. The rest to quarters. Move!

67

They disperse. ESTETE *and the priests remain.*

X

DE SOTO (*to* PIZARRO). Mutiny's smoking. Act now or it'll be a blaze you'll not put out.

PIZARRO. What do I do?

DE SOTO. Take our chances, what else can we do? You have to let him go.

PIZARRO. And what happens then? A tiny army is wiped out in five minutes, and the whole story lost for always. Later someone else will conquer Peru and no one will even remember my name.

DE SOTO. What kind of name will they remember if you kill him?

PIZARRO. A conqueror. That at least.

DE SOTO. A man who butchered his prisoner after giving his word. There's a name for your ballads.

PIZARRO. I'll never live to hear them. What do I care? What does it matter? Whatever I do, what does it matter?

DE SOTO. Nothing, if you don't feel it. But I think you do.

PIZARRO. Let me understand you. As Second in Command, you counsel certain death for this army?

DE SOTO. I'll not counsel his.

PIZARRO. Then you counsel the death of Christ in this country, as you told my page boy months ago?

DE SOTO. That's not known.

PIZARRO. As good.

DE SOTO. No. Christ is love. Love is—

PIZARRO. What? *What?*

DE SOTO. Now in him. He trusts you, trust him. It's all you can do.

PIZARRO. Have you gone soft in the head? What's this chorus now? 'Trust! trust!' You know the law out here: kill or get killed. You said it yourself. The mercies come later.

68

DE SOTO. Not for you. I wish to God you'd never made this bargain. But you did. Now you've no choice left.

PIZARRO. No, this is my kingdom. In Peru I am absolute. I have choice always.

DE SOTO. You had it. But you made it.

PIZARRO. Then I'll take it back.

DE SOTO. Then you never made it. I'm not playing words, General. There's no choice where you don't stick by it.

PIZARRO. I can *choose* to take it back.

DE SOTO. No, sir. That would only be done on orders from your own fear. That's not choosing.

ESTETE. May the Crown be allowed a word?

PIZARRO. I know your word. Death.

ESTETE. What else can it be?

VALVERDE. Your army is in terror. Do you care nothing for them?

PIZARRO. Well, Cavalier. Do you?

DE SOTO. I care for them. But less than I care for you . . . God knows why.

    He goes off.

ESTETE. The issue is simple. You are Viceroy here ruling in the name of the King who sent you. You have no right to risk his land for any reason at all.

PIZARRO. And what did this King ever do for me? Granted me salary if I found money to pay it. Allowed me governance if I found land to govern. Magnificent! For years I strove to make this expedition, years of scars and hunger. While I sweated your Holy Roman vulture turned away his beak till I'd shaken out enough gold to tempt his greed. If I'd failed this time he'd have cast me off with one shrug of his royal feathers. Well, now I cast him. Francisco Pizarro casts off Carlos the Fifth. Go and tell him.

ESTETE. This is ridiculous.

PIZARRO. No doubt, but you'll have to give me better argument before I give him up.

ESTETE. Perverse man, what is Atahuallpa to you?

PIZARRO. Someone I promised Life.

ESTETE. Promised life? How quaint. The sort of chivalry idea you pretend to despise. If you want to be an absolute king, my man, you must learn to act out of personal will. Break your word just *because* you gave it. Till then, you're only a pig-man trying to copy his betters.

PIZARRO *rounds on him angrily.*

VALVERDE. My son, listen to me. No promise to a pagan need bind a Christian. Simply think what's at stake: the lives of a hundred and seventy of the faithful. Are you going to sacrifice them for one savage?

PIZARRO. You know lives have no weight, Father. Ten can't be added up to outbalance one.

VALVERDE. Ten good can against one evil. And this man is evil. His people kiss his hands as the source of life.

PIZARRO. As we do yours. All your days you play at being God. You only hate my Inca because he does it better.

VALVERDE. *What?*

PIZARRO. Dungballs to all churches that are or ever could be! How I hate you. 'Kill who I bid you kill and I will pardon it.' YOU with your milky fingers forcing in the blade. How dare you priests bless any man who goes slicing into battle? But no. You slice with him. 'Rip!' you scream, 'Tear! blind! in the name of Christ!' Tell me soft Father, if Christ was here now, do you think he would kill my Inca? . . . Well, Brother de Nizza, you're the lord of answers: let's hear you. Do I kill him?

DE NIZZA. Don't try and trap me. I know as well as you how terrible it is to kill. But worse is to spare evil. When I came here first I thought I had found Paradise. Now I know it is Hell. A country which castrates its people. What are your Inca's subjects? A population of eunuchs, living entirely without choice.

PIZARRO. And what are your Christians? Unhappy hating men. Look: I'm a peasant, I want value for money. If I go marketing for Gods, who do I buy? The God of Europe with all its death and blooding, or Atahuallpa of Peru?

70

His spirit keeps an Empire sweet and still as corn in the field.

DENIZZA. And you're content to be a stalk of corn?

PIZARRO. Yes, yes! They're no fools, these sun men. They know what cheats you sell on your barrow. Choice. Hunger. Tomorrow. They've looked at your wares and passed on. They live here as part of nature, no hope and no despair.

DENIZZA. And no life. Why must you be so dishonest? You are not only part of nature, and you know it. There is something in you at war with nature; there is in all of us. Something that does not belong in you the animal. What do you think it is? What is this pain in you that month after month makes you hurl yourself against the cage of time? ... This is God, driving you to accept divine eternity. Take it, General: not this pathetic copy of eternity the Incas have tried to make on earth. Peru is a sepulchre of the soul. For the sake of the free spirit in each of us it must be destroyed.

PIZARRO. So there is Christian charity. To save my own soul I must kill another man!

DENIZZA. To save love in the world you must kill lovelessness.

PIZARRO. Hail to you, sole judge of love! No salvation outside your church: and no love neither. Oh, you arrogance! ... (*Simply*) I do not know love, Father, but what can I ever know, if I feel none for him?

DIEGO (*rushing on*). Sir! Sir!
Another fight broke out, sir. There's one dead.

PIZARRO. Who?

DIEGO. Blas. He drew a knife. I only meant to spit his leg, but he slipped and got it through the guts.

PIZARRO. You did well to punish fighting.

DIEGO. May I speak free, sir?

PIZARRO. What? I've got to kill him, is that it?

DIEGO. What other way is there? The men are out of their wits. They feel death all round them.

PIZARRO. So it is and let them face it. I promised them gold, not life. Well, they've got gold. The cripples have gold

71

crutches. The coughers spit gold snot. The bargain's over.

DIEGO. No, sir, not with me. To me you're the greatest General in the world. And we're the greatest company.

PIZARRO. Pizarro's boys, is that it?

DIEGO. Yes, sir. Pizarro's boys.

PIZARRO. Ah, the old band. The dear old regiment. Fool! Look, you were born a man. Not a Blue man, or a Green man, but A MAN. You are able to feel a thousand separate loves unordered by fear or solitude. Are you going to trade them all in for Gang-love? Flag-love? Carlos-the-Fifth-love? Jesus-the-Christ-love? All that has been tied on you; it is only this that makes you bay for death.

VALVERDE. I'll give you death. When I get back to Spain, a commission will hale you to the stake for what you have said today.

PIZARRO. If I let the Inca go, Father, you'll never get back to Spain.

ESTETE. You madman: see here, you put him underground by sunset or I'll take the knife to him myself.

PIZARRO. ATAHUALLPA!

ATAHUALLPA *enters with* YOUNG MARTIN.

They ache for your death. They want to write psalms to their God in your blood. But they'll all die before you – that I promise. (*He binds* ATAHUALLPA'S *arm to his own with a long cord of rope last used to tie some gold.*) There. No, no, some here. Now no one will kill you unless they kill me first.

ESTETE. De Candia!

Enter DE CANDIA, *with a drawn sword.*

DE CANDIA. A touching game – gaolers and prisoners. But it's over now. General, do you think I'm going to die so that you can dance with a darkie?

PIZARRO *pulls the sword from* YOUNG MARTIN'S *scabbard.*

DIEGO (*drawing*). Sorry sir, but it's got to be done.

ESTETE (*drawing*). There's nothing you can do, Pizarro. The whole camp's against you.

PIZARRO. De Soto!

DE CANDIA. If de Soto raises his sword, he'll lose the arm that swings it.

PIZARRO. You'll lose yours first. Come on!

He rushes at DE CANDIA *but* ATAHUALLPA *gives a growl and pulls him back by the rope. A pause.*

ATAHUALLPA. I have no eyes for you. You are nothing.

PIZARRO. I command here still. They will obey me.

ATAHUALLPA. They will kill me though you cry curses of earth and sky. (*To them all*) Leave us. I will speak with him.

Impressed by the command in his voice, all leave, save the General – now roped to his prisoner – and YOUNG MARTIN.

XI

ATAHUALLPA. It is no matter.   hey cannot kill me.

PIZARRO. Cannot?

ATAHUALLPA. Man who dies cannot kill a God who lives forever.

PIZARRO. I wouldn't bet on it, my lord.

ATAHUALLPA. Only my father can take me from here. And he would not accept me killed by men like you. Men with no word. You may be King in this land, but never God. I am God of the Four Quarters and if you kill me tonight I will rise at dawn when my Father first touches my body with light.

PIZARRO. You believe this?

ATAHUALLPA. All my people know it – it is why they have let me stay with you.

PIZARRO. They knew you could not be harmed . . .

ATAHUALLPA. So.

PIZARRO. Was this the meaning? The meaning of my dream? You were choosing me?

YOUNG MARTIN. My lord, it's just a boast. Beyond any kind of reason.

PIZARRO. Is it?

73

YOUNG MARTIN. How can a man die, then get up and walk away?

PIZARRO. Let's hear your creed, boy. 'I believe in Jesus Christ, the Son of God, that He suffered under Pontius Pilate, was crucified, dead and buried' . . . and what?

YOUNG MARTIN. Sir?

PIZARRO. What?

YOUNG MARTIN. 'He descended into Hell, and on the third day He rose again from the dead . . .'

PIZARRO. You don't believe it!

YOUNG MARTIN. I do! On my soul! I believe with perfect faith!

PIZARRO. But Christ's to be the only one, is that it? What if it's possible, here in a land beyond all maps and scholars, guarded by mountains up to the sky, that there were true Gods on earth, creator of true peace? Think of it! Gods, free of time.

YOUNG MARTIN. It's impossible, my lord.

PIZARRO. It's the only way to give life meaning! To blast out of time and live forever, *us*, in our own persons. This is the law: die in despair or be a God yourself! . . . Look at him: always so calm as if the teeth of life never bit him . . . or the teeth of death. What if it was really true, Martin? That I've gone God-hunting and caught one. A being who can renew his life over and over?

YOUNG MARTIN. But how can he do that, sir? How could any man?

PIZARRO. By returning over and over again to the source of life – *to the Sun*!

YOUNG MARTIN. No, sir . . .

PIZARRO. Why not? What else is a God but what we know we can't do without? The flowers that worship it, the sun-flowers in their soil, are us after night, after cold and light-less days, turning our faces to it, adoring. The sun is the only God I know! We eat you to walk. We drink you to sing. Our reins loosen under you and we laugh. Even I laugh, here!

YOUNG MARTIN. General, you need rest, sir.

Pause.

PIZARRO. Yes. Yes . . . yes. (*Bitterly*) How clever. He's understood everything I've said to him these awful months – all the secret pain he's heard – and this is his revenge. This futile joke. How he must hate me. (*Tightening the rope*) Oh, yes, you cunning bastard! Look, Martin – behold, my God. I've got the Sun on a string! I can make it rise: (*He pulls the Inca's arm up*) – or set! *He throws the Inca to his knees.*

YOUNG MARTIN. General . . . !

PIZARRO. I'll make you set forever! Two can joke as well as one. You want your freedom? All right, you're Free! (*He starts circling round* ATAHUALLPA) Walk out of the camp! They may stop you, but what's that to you? You're invulnerable. They'll knock you down but your father the Sun will pick you up again. Go on! Get up! . . . Go on! . . . Get up! . . . Go on! . . . Go on! . . . Go on! . . . Go on! . . . Go on! . . . Go on!

He breaks into a frantic gallop round and round the Inca, the rope at full stretch, ATAHUALLPA *turning with him, somersaulting, then holding him, his teeth bared with the strain, as if breaking a wild horse, until the old man tumbles exhausted to the ground. Silence follows, broken only by deep moaning from the stricken man. Quietly the Inca pulls in the rope. Then at last he speaks.*

ATAHUALLPA. Pizarro. You will die soon and you do not believe in your God. That is why you tremble and keep no word. Believe in me. I will give you a word and fill you with joy. For you I will do a great thing. I will swallow death and spit it out of me.

Pause. This whole scene stays very still.

PIZARRO (*whispering*). You cannot.

ATAHUALLPA. Yes, if my father wills it.

PIZARRO. How if he does not?

ATAHUALLPA. He will. His people still need me. Believe.

PIZARRO. Impossible.

ATAHUALLPA. Believe.

G 75

PIZARRO. How? . . . How? . . .

ATAHUALLPA. First you must take my priest power.

PIZARRO (*quietly*). Oh, no! you go or not as you choose, but I take nothing more in this world.

ATAHUALLPA. Take my word. Take my peace. I will put water to your wound, old man. Believe.

A long silence. The lights are now fading round them.

PIZARRO. What must I do?

Enter OLD MARTIN.

OLD MARTIN. How can I speak now and hope to be believed? As night fell like a hand over the eye, and great white stars sprang out over the snow-rim of our world, Atahuallpa confessed Pizarro. He did it in the Inca manner. He took Ichu grass and a stone. Into the Ichu grass the General spoke for an hour or more. None heard what he said save the King, who could not understand it. Then the King struck him on the back with the stone, cast away the grass, and made the signs for purification.

PIZARRO. If any blessing is in me, take it and go. Fly up, my bird, and come to me again.

The INCA *takes a knife from* YOUNG MARTIN *and cuts the rope. Then he walks upstage. All the* OFFICERS *and* MEN *enter. During the following a pole is set up above, in the sun, and* ATAHUALLPA *is hauled up into it.*

XII

OLD MARTIN. The Inca was tried by a court quickly mustered. He was accused of usurping the throne and killing his brother; of idolatry and of having more than one wife. On all these charges he was found—

ESTETE. Guilty.

VALVERDE. Guilty.

DE CANDIA. Guilty.

DIEGO. Guilty.

76

OLD MARTIN. Sentence to be carried out the same night.

ESTETE. Death by burning.

Lights up above the sun.

ATAHUALLPA *gives a great cry.*

PIZARRO. No! He must not burn! His body must stay in one piece.

VALVERDE. Let him repent his idolatry and be baptized a Christian. He will receive the customary mercy.

OLD MARTIN. Strangling instead.

PIZARRO. You must do it! Deny your Father! If you don't, you will be burnt to ashes. There will be no flesh left for him to warm alive at dawn.

YOUNG MARTIN *screams and runs from the stage in horror.*

You must do it.

In a gesture of surrender the Inca king kneels.

OLD MARTIN. So it was that Atahuallpa came to Christ.

Enter DE NIZZA, *above, with a bowl of water.*

DE NIZZA. I baptise you Juan de Atahuallpa, in honour of Juan the Baptist, whose sacred day this is.

ESTETE. The twenty-ninth of August 1533.

VALVERDE. And may Our Lord and His angels receive your soul with joy!

SOLDIERS. Amen!

The Inca suddenly raises his head, tears off his clothes and intones in a great voice:

ATAHUALLPA. INTI! INTI! INTI!

VALVERDE. What does he say?

PIZARRO (*intoning also*). The Sun. The Sun. The Sun.

VALVERDE. *Kill him!*

Soldiers haul ATAHUALLPA *to his feet and hold him to the stake.* RODAS *slips a string over his head and while all the Spaniards recite the Latin Creed below, and great howls of 'Inca!' come from the darkness, the Sovereign King of Peru is garrotted. His screams and struggles subside; his body falls slack. His executioners hand the corpse down to the soldiers below, who carry it to the centre of the stage and drop*

77

it at PIZARRO'S *feet. Then all leave save the old man, who stands as if turned to stone. A drum beats. Slowly, in semi-darkness, the stage fills with all the Indians, robed in black and terracotta, wearing the great golden funeral masks of ancient Peru. Grouped round the prone body, they intone a strange Chant of Resurrection, punctuated by hollow beats on the drums and by long, long silences in which they turn their immense triangular eyes enquiringly up to the sky. Finally, after three great cries appear to summon it, the sun rises. Its rays fall on the body.* ATA-HUALLPA *does not move. The masked men watch in amazement – disbelief – finally, despair. Slowly, with hanging, dejected heads, they shuffle away.* PIZARRO *is left alone with the dead King. He contemplates him. A silence. Then suddenly he slaps it viciously, and the body rolls over on its back.*

PIZARRO. Cheat! You've cheated me! Cheat . . .

For a moment his old body is racked with sobs; then, surprised, he feels tears on his cheek. He examines them. The sunlight brightens on his head.

What's this? What is it? In all your life you never made one of these, I know, and I not till this minute. Look. (*He kneels to show the dead Inca*) Ah, no. You have no eyes for me now, Atahuallpa: they are dusty balls of amber I can tap on. You have no peace for me, Atahuallpa: the birds still scream in your forest. You have no joy for me, Atahuallpa, my boy: the only joy is in death. I lived between two hates: I die between two darks: blind eyes and a blind sky. And yet you saw once. The sky sees nothing, but you saw. Is their comfort there? The sky knows no feeling, but we know them, that's sure. Martin's hope, and de Soto's honour, and your trust – your trust which hunted me: we alone make these. That's some marvel, yes, some marvel. To sit in a great cold silence, and sing out sweet with just our own warm breath: that's some marvel, surely. To make water in a sand world: surely, surely . . . God's just a name on your nail; and naming begins cries and cruelties. But to live without hope of after, and make whatever God there is, oh, that's some immortal business surely . . . I'm tired. Where are you? You're so cold. I'd warm you if I could. But there's no warming now, not ever now. I'm colding too. There's a snow of death falling all round us. You can almost see it. It's over, lad, I'm coming after you. There's nothing but peace to come. We'll be put into the same earth, father and son in our own land. And that sun will roam uncaught over his empty pasture.

OLD MARTIN. So fell Peru. We gave her greed, hunger and the Cross: three gifts for the civilized life. The family groups that sang on the terraces are gone. In their place slaves shuffle underground and they don't sing there. Peru is a silent country, frozen in avarice. So fell Spain, gorged with gold; distended; now dying.

PIZARRO (*singing*). 'Where is her heart, O little finch' . . .

OLD MARTIN. And so fell you, General, my master, whom men called the Son of His Own Deeds. He was killed later in a quarrel with his partner who brought up the reinforcements. But to speak truth, he sat down that morning and never really got up again.

PIZARRO (*singing*). 'Where are her plumes, O little finch' . . .

OLD MARTIN. I'm the only one left now of that company: landowner – slaveowner – and forty years from any time of hope. It put out a good blossom, but it was shaken off rough. After that I reckon the fruit always comes sour, and doesn't sweeten up much with age.

PIZARRO (*singing*). 'She is cut up, O little finch. For stealing grain, O little finch' . . .

OLD MARTIN. General, you did for me, and now I've done for you. And there's no joy in that. Or in anything now. But then there's no joy in the world could match for me what I had when I first went with you across the water to find the gold country. And no pain like losing it. Save you all.

He goes out. PIZARRO *lies beside the body of*

79

INTRODUCTION

I. THE AUTHOR

Peter Levin Shaffer was born on 15 May 1926 and educated at St Paul's School, London, and Trinity College, Cambridge. He started playwriting soon after leaving Cambridge, but his first successes were television productions, *Balance of Terror* and *The Salt Lands*. His first major stage production, *Five Finger Exercise*, appeared in the West End in 1958. On the surface, this play seems to rely on traditional formulae. It is set in a prosperous middle-class drawing room and features a group of five traditional characters. But Shaffer penetrates below appearances and faces his characters with a new situation which disturbs their traditional relationships. His other characteristics as revealed in this play are skilful construction and articulate, explicit dialogue, while a distinguishing feature is its impersonality – the apparent lack of favouritism in the author's treatment of his characters.

Shaffer's next works to be staged were two one-act plays, *The Private Ear* and *The Public Eye*. The former is set in a bedsitter and concerns the relations between two young men and a girl. The milieu this time is lower middle-class, and the characterisation less convincing than in *Five Finger Exercise*. But, technically, the play shows Shaffer's stage sense, especially in the skilful way sound effects are used both structurally and to underline emotion. *The Public Eye* concerns a pompous and dull chartered accountant, his wife whom he wrongly suspects of infidelity, and an eccentric private detective whom the accountant has hired and who brings about a reunion in the end. Again, the play is clever and witty, but there is little in Shaffer's work so far to foreshadow publicly anything as ambitious as *The Royal Hunt of the Sun*, which, though already written, had not yet been produced. The reasons for its delayed production were the demands it made on resources and the huge cast required. Written for the Royal Shakespeare Theatre Company at the Aldwych Theatre, it was finally bought by Sir Laurence

Olivier for the National Theatre and first performed at the Chichester Festival Theatre on 7 July 1964.

Shaffer's other works include *The Prodigal Father* (a radio play), *The Merry Roosters' Panto*, and a farce called *Black Comedy*, which opened at Chichester on 27 July 1965.

II. The Play

THEMES

The *Royal Hunt of the Sun* is described as 'a play concerning the Conquest of Peru'. The vastness of this subject brings it into sharp contrast with Shaffer's preceding works. Since the story involves the clash of two different civilizations, the author is enabled to draw comparisons and expound on their relative virtues and vices. In a programme note, he declares his intention to depict 'an encounter between European hope and Indian hopelessness; between Indian faith and European faithlessness. I saw the active iron of Spain against the passive feathers of Peru: the conflict of two immense and joyless powers. The Spaniards suspected joy as being unworthy of Christ. The Peruvian could hardly know it, since in his wholly organized world he was forbidden despair. The Conquistadors deified personal will: the Incas shunned it.'

The play is based on a nineteenth century historical classic, *The Conquest of Peru*, by W. H. Prescott, and in the broad outline of the story and in many of its details, Shaffer follows Prescott closely. But a comparison of the play with the source book shows that Shaffer deviated in certain particulars, to serve the requirements of dramatic construction and also his own personal preoccupations. By modifying the character of Pizarro and the motives of Atahuallpa, he was able to explore the dilemma of a man who has lost his faith in conventional religion, but has as yet found no satisfactory substitute. Pizarro can see no point in loving and trusting in a universe where the only things he is certain of are time and death, which destroy everything and make human effort pointless.

His 'hunt' in this play is less for gold and power than for a set of satisfactory beliefs and values by which to live. Through Pizarro, Shaffer questions all ideals, all slogans, all excuses for simplifying life, all ways in which man 'trivialises the immensity of his experiences'.

Shaffer's concern with the need for love is not new in his work. The definition of love voiced by a character in *The Public Eye*, 'Love is a great burst of joy that someone exists', is applicable, with slight modification, to the experience of Pizarro at the end of *The Royal Hunt of the Sun*.

III. Dramatic Qualities: General

The Royal Hunt of the Sun involves both the drama of a clash of two nations and a personal drama. The play succeeds best when the confrontation between Pizarro and Atahuallpa is the centre of interest, mainly in the second part. Here the larger forces in the background claim attention only in so far as they shape the personal drama and press the protagonists in a particular direction. These forces are the soldiers' lust for gold and desire for safety to enjoy it, the concern of the churchmen to effect a conversion or to extend their dominion, the anxiety of the King's overseer to make sure Carlos the Fifth gets his due. What fascinates Pizarro about the Inca civilization is that its members appear to have escaped from time by escaping from change; they have also, by submitting to a strict routine laid down for them, escaped the need to struggle and make decisions.

As well as having strong theatrical appeal, this play is thought-provoking. The clash of the two systems sometimes takes the form of intellectual debate, but clever though this is, it tends to be less absorbing than the personal drama. The contrast between the two systems remains mostly on an abstract level, since for stage purposes the dramatic conflict must be more between Spaniards and Indians as human beings than between the concepts of free will and submission to authority. The Spaniards, although they contemplate mutiny, seem almost as thoroughly conditioned in their own way as the Indians. The two systems as systems never seem to come into dramatic conflict.

The balance of the debate is also in question. The Roman Catholic position is constantly attacked and defeated, mainly by Pizarro but also by Villac Umu, Atahuailpa, and finally by Martin, who has the last word. Failing to preserve the detachment of earlier plays, Shaffer allows Pizarro to become his mouthpiece, and the propaganda runs away with the play on occasions.

This is not to say that we are never aware of Pizarro's personal emotions. The scenes between Pizarro and Atahuallpa are, at times, very affecting. If the points of similarity which they discover – their illegitimacy, their both being thieves – seem inadequate as a basis for love, for a man like the Pizarro of the play even such points of contact with another human being as these represents progress.

The end of the play is moving and in some degree tragic. True, Atahuallpa dies happy and Pizarro affirms his faith in human feelings, but Pizarro's awakening comes too late for him to save the object of his love. Whatever he decides, Atahuallpa will die. Pizarro comes into the play in the frame of mind Shakespeare's Macbeth reached at the end of his life; nothing satisfies, nothing signifies. He has been blighted and warped many years before. Pizarro is trapped, but he does attain the stature of a tragic hero faced by uncontrollable forces. But he, also, is destroyed. Old Martin tells us Pizarro's life ended with the death of Atahuallpa, and the consequences of his actions, which are of epic magnitude, are pitilessly exposed.

IV. THE CHARACTERS

PIZARRO

The most important character in the play is Pizarro. At one point he sees himself as a conqueror of the stature of Tamburlaine and Alexander, but Shaffer does not concentrate on this aspect of him. Magnificent as his achievements are, Pizarro interests the author mainly because of his personal dilemma.

Pizarro is a man with a grievance, a man wounded by the circumstances of his birth. The physical wound which he had acquired on a previous expedition takes on symbolic overtones in this play. The illiterate, underprivileged pig-boy is sensitive to taunts about his mean origins, as is shown by the way Estete manages to hurt him. When he accuses Pizarro of being merely 'a pig-man trying to copy his betters', Pizarro 'rounds on him angrily'. To overcome this disadvantage, Pizarro seeks a name, a reputation, recognition from the unfair society of his native land. The way for him is through foreign conquest and gold. He has natural qualities which favour him. He is a strong leader who fearlessly asserts his leadership against the high-born Estete and rules his men with a rod of iron. But his own life has forced him to the conclusion that the world is a jungle, and he has therefore cultivated only those qualities, ruthlessness and unscrupulousness, which will allow him to compete. 'Don't trust me,' he tells Young Martin, 'or I'll hurt you beyond believing.'

In the play, however, Pizarro is not merely a seeker after success and reputation. To become a legend is a means of living on after death. Pizarro is a man who has lost his religious faith; he is an agnostic seeking for something to take the sting out of death. Perhaps this forces Shaffer to make his hero rather more philosophic and articulate than one would expect. Perhaps, also, from the point of view of dramatic development, he repeats his disillusionment too often.

But towards the end of the play his growing attachment to Atahuallpa makes it more difficult for him to reject with his customary callousness the arguments in favour of principle and trust put forward by de Soto, Young Martin, and Atahuallpa. Shaffer places immediate responsibility for the execution on the shoulders of others, and the important fact is that Pizarro has made progress as a person. He finds communion with another human being, he discovers feelings in himself which surprise him; Atahuallpa moves him to laughter and tears, and to a measure of joy. In a sense, the bitter blow which the god's death inflicts on the new convert to the

Inca faith is not completely catastrophic. Although he has lost the object of his affections, he has gained solace from the fact that such affections exist.

Pizarro is a piece of intriguing and, on the whole, successful characterisation. His personal attractiveness for the playwright is both a strength and a weakness. At best he provides the focus for all the themes of the play; at worst he either becomes a mouthpiece for the author or fails to communicate the personal grief he describes, or which is referred to by others.

ATAHUALLPA

The Atahuallpa in the play in many ways parallels that of Prescott. 'He is allowed,' says Prescott, 'to have been bold, high-minded and liberal. All agree that he showed singular penetration and quickness of perception. His exploits as a warrior had placed his valour beyond dispute.' Shaffer's Inca has high principles and treats the Spaniards in a courteous and trusting manner, but, when betrayed, he quickly grasps that whatever they may profess, the true object of their desires is gold. His skill in fighting is demonstrated in his duel with Pizarro.

One important feature for which Shaffer finds warrant in Prescott is the Inca's coldness and aloofness towards inferiors. His Atahuallpa shows his self-will when he disregards the warnings of his advisers. For Shaffer's purposes, though, it is the Inca's 'lovelessness' that has to be stressed, as he has to learn love through his encounter with Pizarro. But his unwillingness to show mercy towards the murderers of Cajamarca, if he is freed, seems, in the context, a matter of simple justice. One might point to the casual way he is prepared to sacrifice his priests or to the murder of his own brother, but with the example of the professedly enlightened Christians before us, even this does not seem uniquely callous. Pizarro shares with Atahuallpa this quality of detachment, of 'lovelessness', but in Pizarro's case it is more extensively and convincingly present.

Introduction

In *The Royal Hunt of the Sun*, Atahuallpa becomes a substitute for the Christ of the Spaniards. His death reminds one of the Crucifixion. The difference is that Atahuallpa makes his conquest by *not* rising from the dead. In failing to justify Pizarro's false hopes, he breaks his heart, but shows him the way to true acceptance and peace. Shaffer gives Atahuallpa nobler motives than Prescott attributes to him. In Prescott's book he dies bravely and stoically as befits an Indian warrior; in the play he performs an act of love.

OTHER CHARACTERS

Compared with Pizarro and Atahuallpa, none of the other characters is fully realized. Martin is primarily a narrative device. As a 'character' he represents the adult and youthful versions of one and the same person. He is thus a means whereby both the excitement of youthful idealism and its fallaciousness and vulnerability can be presented. As Martin says at the end: 'But then there's no joy in the world could match for me what I had when I first went with you across the water to find the gold country. And no pain like losing it.' Pizarro himself eventually accepts Martin's hope as one of the things that gives human life nobility. For most of the play, though, the Young Martin exists to throw Pizarro's cynicism into relief, and to point out his lack of principle over the treatment of Atahuallpa.

The Cavalier de Soto, although he is less static than the remaining characters, is also nearer to a useful device than an independent person. He is a confidant, someone to whom Pizarro can unlock his secret thoughts. For the first part of the play he puts conventional views. He is staunchly for Spain and for Christ, and even shares the views of his contemporary Christians on the necessity for killing in order to establish the Kingdom of Love, as he tells the nauseated Young Martin. Later Shaffer changes him and we find him acting as the personal conscience of Pizarro and advising him not to kill Atahuallpa, even if it means the death of Christ in the land. Here Shaffer skilfully alters Prescott also, as Pres-

87

cott's Pizarro was unprincipled enough to send de Soto on an expedition to keep him from interfering. But Shaffer attempts to make the later de Soto psychologically convincing, and to do so gives him motives for his new attitudes. De Soto is so friendly towards Pizarro that Pizarro's welfare is all he cares about; his association with him has given him insights into his basic needs. From the reader's point of view, however, these motives need to be given greater emphasis.

The other characters are generalized and unchanging; simplified types representing points of view. Within their limits, though, they are differentiated. Valverde, the Dominican, is harsh, bullying and hypocritical. His professed aim is the conversion of the heathen, but his secret aim is power. As Pizarro says: 'All your days you play at being God. You only hate my Inca because he does it better.' His approach to conversion is, by preference, through force. 'Show them rigour,' he says. He confines his blessing to those who have accepted the Faith. He lacks intelligence and is constantly defeated in argument, replying to a palpable hit with abuse: 'You are being deliberately stupid,' for example, or 'This is the Devil's tongue.'

De Nizza, on the other hand, is a mild Franciscan who is more quietly reasonable than Valverde and wishes to coax the Indian to salvation. He makes out a better case for Christianity, although his belief in the necessity of suffering leads him to defend want and hunger, and on this point Shaffer gives the victory to Pizarro. De Nizza also counsels the death of Atahuallpa and on this point, also, his reasoning is suspect:

PIZARRO. To save my own soul I must kill another man.
DE NIZZA. To save love in the world you must kill lovelessness.
PIZARRO. Hail to you, sole judge of love!

But he is allowed shrewdly to enumerate the weaknesses of the Inca view of life and even to point out the inadequacy of that philosophy for Pizarro.

Apart from the wry and cynical de Candia, the arrogant, grasping King's man, Estete, and Felipillo, who acts out Shaf-

88

fer's description of him, the rest of the characters are pale and barely distinguishable, the greedy Spaniards lively as a group, but the Indians very shadowy.

V Form and Structure

The Royal Hunt of the Sun is a chronicle play in that it records actual historical events, and an example of epic theatre in so far as these events are of major political and social importance and are dealt with on a large scale. As such it represents a complete change from Shaffer's previous stage plays, which had involved small casts and single, contemporary localities. To suit his epic needs, Shaffer's professed aim in this play was 'total theatre', in which not merely dialogue but many other elements should be used. He wanted to create 'an experience that was entirely and only theatrical'. Whether he succeeds in this remains to be examined, but certainly the result of the effort is a disciplined spectacle which provides a kind of excitement rare in modern plays.

Apart from dialogue, then, Shaffer uses elements some of which are of great antiquity. Mime, which was used in the Chinese and Indian theatres, is, for example, included here to show the crossing of the Andes by Pizarro's men. More suitably, perhaps, there is the miming of the work by the Indians which, helped by a toil song, emphasises their ritualistic, mechanical lives. The mime of the great massacre combines with a simple dance in most effectively showing the waves of Indians being inexorably slaughtered. Chanting between Atahuallpa and his priests stresses the formality of the relationship. In the original production of the play, there was even the appearance of a god in a machine – the mechanical sun which unfolds before us; a device such as would have delighted the Greeks. Shaffer also makes use of masks, most effectively in the scene at the end, where the priests surround the body of the Inca, waiting for the sun to rise and the god to return to life. In production, these masks, with their huge eyes, are disturbingly impressive as the sun slowly lights them and they sway to and fro expressing the bewilderment and despair of a nation. Masks had already been made familiar by other modern playwrights, including Bertolt Brecht, the German writer.

Also in common with other contemporary playwrights, Shaffer in this play advocates the abandonment of naturalistic scenery. The sun device in the Chichester and Old Vic productions serves many purposes, but Shaffer stresses that even this is not necessary, and that 'essentially all that is required . . . is a bare stage and an upper level'. This, as we shall see, gives the action considerable flexibility. The use of theatrical symbolism is often a convenient short cut for stage purposes, and the bloodstained cloth in this play, which is an attempt at symbolic effect, hardly justifies itself, especially as the emission of the sun's blood has already been described in words.

In other respects, though, Shaffer's use of technical resources is lavish. He makes great play with lighting and sound effects, suggesting trees with mottled patterns and the murderous jungle with stereophonic bird cries. These devices make vividly present on the stage the metaphorical jungle, in terms of which Pizarro sees the world. The costumes realize Shaffer's conception of the conflict between 'the active iron of Spain' and 'the passive feathers of Peru'.

Yet another epic device which serves the epic scope of the theme is the narrator, Martin Ruiz. He fills in the story and allows the author to take short cuts at opportune moments. Thus at Cajamarca he records the passing of ten hours and, at the entrance of the Inca, allows the dramatic tension to continue uninterrupted when he saves us from having to listen to Valverde expounding the Christian faith. His substitution for Felipillo as interpreter aids convenience without violating psychological credibility.

Martin's function is, of course, not merely structural. Being a split-image device, he is both involved in and detached from events. Thus when he says 'That night, as I knelt vomiting into a canal, the empire of the Incas stopped. The spring of the clock was snapped. For a thousand miles men sat down not knowing what to do', we have both the immediate reaction of Young Martin and a comment by an adult, reflecting on the event with full consciousness of its drama and its historical significance.

Shaffer chooses to unfold his epic theme by using a succession of episodes rather than long scenes. The relevance of this method to a conflict between two nations is obvious. The switching between the Christian camp and the Indian, setting the Inca's trust against the rapacity of the invaders, creates dramatic irony, sometimes made more effective by the starkness of the juxtaposition. At the end of Act I, Scene iii, Atahuallpa says: 'If the White God comes to bless me, all must see him,' but immediately, with the beginning of the next scene, a 'horde of Indians rushes across the stage' and de Candia says, 'Grab that one! That's the chief. Now you brownie bastard, show us gold.' Sometimes Martin links the scenes, but even here his comments often gain effect through sharp contrast. In Act II the protagonists, together now, are forming an attachment and leave the stage hand in hand, but the vulnerability of this relationship is dramatically pointed by Old Martin's next speech: 'Slowly the pile increased. The army waited nervously and licked its lips. Greed began to rise in us like a tide of sea.'

The unchanging stage set allows Shaffer, in Act I, to juxtapose effectively speeches spoken in different localities within the same scene. Atahuallpa remains in the background on the upper stage during some of the 'Spanish' scenes. The fact of his constant interest in the invaders is thus theatrically emphasized, and through the dovetailing of his and Pizarro's speeches an effect equivalent to the *montage* of camera shots is achieved. At one point, a relatively dull patch of exposition is startlingly enlivened when the officially invisible Inca seems to be about to materialize in front of Pizarro.

HEADMAN. So he has eyes everywhere. He sees you now.
PIZARRO. Now?
ATAHUALLPA. Now!

Instead, Challcuchima makes a shock entry.

H   91

Viewing the dramatic development of the play as a whole, many critics have agreed that Act I is disappointing and Act II absorbing. Certainly the central interest lies in the scenes between Pizarro and Atahuallpa. When in a play the roots of the story are to be found in previous history, the author faces the difficult task of bringing the audience up to date, of telling them enough of the background to make sense of the action. Shaffer makes Martin record the actual dates when important scenes took place. Thus the audience is reminded that it is watching historical events, credible because of the particular setting in which they took place. So, with better grace, we can accept such fantastic events as Pizarro's conversion to the Inca faith.

Unfortunately, the exposition in this play does at times slow up the development. Useful though Martin is, his direct method of recording facts seems more appropriate to a novel than a play. He recounts Pizarro's previous journeys and fills in the details about characters such as Almagro, who is unimportant in this play. Then, of course, we have to be told all about Peruvian society and its engineering feats, but these sections are rather undramatic.

The trouble seems to be that Pizarro's unique problem is not introduced until late in the Act, so that the relevance of some of the background is not clear at the time. At first, Pizarro is not distinguished by any very interesting motives. He seeks gold and power as do most of the others. He has a conflict with Estete, and disagreements with Martin and Valverde. But he does not really become interesting as a person until the scene with de Soto, where he confesses his dream and his personal need to meet the sun-god. From then onwards, the encounter between the two men takes on a new meaning.

Another 'formal' characteristic of this play is that Shaffer presents not merely a story, but also a clash of two systems. His tendency to treat this clash in terms of general ideas leads him occasionally to write in a way that reminds the reader of Bernard Shaw, and particularly, the theme being what it is, of *Saint Joan*. Sometimes the action stops or slows down to give way to debate, as, for example, when the Christian priests and the Indians discuss their rival religions, or when de Candia and Estete argue the rival merits of Venice and Spain. At times, too, a set speech, such as that Pizarro produces on legitimacy is reminiscent of those speeches in Shaw's plays which have some of the characteristics of an aria in opera. The way Pizarro tends to state his motives at the beginning of the play rather than leaving it to the audience to infer them, may also seem to resemble Shaw, though direct self-revelation to the audience goes back beyond Shaw to Shakespeare and earlier.

Sometimes Shaffer's penchant for dialectical argument, or perhaps more particularly his desire to put across his own views, adversely affects the tempo of the drama. The long argument of Pizarro with de Nizza, Valverde, Estete and the 'men' before the trial of Atahuallpa tends to focus our attention on the brilliance with which he rebuffs their blandishments and threats rather than on the personal agony which is the result of his growing love for Atahuallpa. Pizarro becomes Shaffer's eloquent and repetitive mouthpiece and the pace slackens.

VI THE WORDS

One can claim for almost any play that it would benefit by being well produced on a stage, but Shaffer aims to create an experience that is 'only theatrical'. That is to say, the stage performance is not merely an attempt to bring the meaning of the words to life in the fullest possible way, it also reveals significant elements for which there is no equivalent in the dialogue. But I think Shaffer is being unfair to his own work if he denies the central importance of the text. In an article in *Plays and Players*, February 1965, Martin Esslin puts the case in an extreme form: 'I personally have no doubt that in fact *The Royal Hunt of the Sun*, greatly though it benefits from excellent design and choreography, is above all a first rate text: witty, wise and well written: if it owes much to its being total theatre (mime, dancing, chanting, ritual) it is the basic conception, the text, which evokes these effects: and the visual effects would be nothing without the text.'

Just how well written is the text of *The Royal Hunt of the Sun*? I think it shows that Shaffer does some things well and others less well. In previous plays, his lively, well-constructed dialogue had been one of his strong points, but in this play he attempts something more, the direct rendering of the powerful emotions and grand conceptions of epic characters, a task that would have excited an Elizabethan dramatist such as Marlowe. But whereas in Elizabethan times the language available had freshness, forcefulness and suggestiveness adequate to the task, that available to Shaffer is flat by comparison.

Pizarro dreams of power as Doctor Faustus did: 'Follow the pig-boy to his glory! I'll have an Empire for my farm. A million boys driving in the pigs at night. And each one of you will own a share – juicy black earth a hundred mile apiece – and golden ploughs to cut it with,' but the thrilling vision is not evoked. Similarly, when he utters his grandiose threats: 'I'll grab you by the legs, you Son of the Sun, and smash your flaming crown on the rocks' Shaffer appears to strain for effect.

Atahuallpa fares no better. Diego's 'Oh look, *look*. God Almighty: it's not happening' is a poor substitute for an evocative description of the Inca's appearance. Nor does the predictable imagery of Atahuallpa's own *cri de-coeur* from his humiliating prison do justice to his feelings: 'Put up a mountain of gold and free your Sun from his prison of clouds.'

When Pizarro's emotion takes the form of bitter cynicism in the diatribe against Spain in Act I, Scene i, the rhetoric is more successful and the formal structure allows him to make his points with force. In fact Shaffer's prose makes a good vehicle for incisive dialectical argument and repartee. Here the tendency is towards the neatness of epigram; for example: 'The world of soldiers is a yard of ungrowable children,' or towards the patterned interchanges of the Indians and the Christian priests.

Possibly the most memorable pieces of writing in the play

are the descriptive passages, as in the following (of the Andes): 'Picture a curtain of stone hung by some giant across your path. Mountains set on mountains: cliffs on cliffs. Hands of rock a hundred yards high with flashing nails where the snow never moved, scratching the gashed face of the sun'; and in this description of the great ascent: 'Four days slowly, like flies, on a wall; limping flies, dying flies, up an endless wall of rock. A tiny army lost in the creases of the moon.' These have weight enough not to need the accompanying lighting and mime to make them live in the imagination. The drama of the waiting in Cajamarca depends on Martin's words for its power.

On the whole the simple and direct statements seem more successful than the attempts at the grand manner. When Martin tells us 'The spring of the clock was snapped', the nature of the Indian society and the simplicity of its destruction are neatly summarized. Dry directness is characteristic of much of Martin's storytelling: 'This story is about ruin. Ruin and gold.' Pizarro reveals his heart with a simple cry: 'O lad, what am I going to do with you?' while in another mood his terse, bare appraisal of a situation – 'We're not fighting ten thousand or three. One man: that's all. Get him, the rest collapse' – shows Shaffer's grasp of effective stage dialogue. Sometimes it is the exactly chosen word which impresses. A whore describes Pizarro as 'frostbitten'; Domingo complains, 'I'm starting to rust.'

Lastly, the success of the tough, terse dialogue among the lower orders of Spanish society, the brutal, greedy soldiery, is notable. At times, Shaffer manages to combine the rhythms of speech with his characteristic formality and sense of design. Pizarro recruits his followers:

PIZARRO. Who's smith here?
SALINAS. I am.
PIZARRO. Are you with us?
SALINAS. I'm not against you.
PIZARRO. Who's your friend?
RODAS. Tailor, if it's your business.

95

Introduction

PIZARRO. Soldiers never stop mending and patching. They'll be grateful for your assistance.

RODAS. We'll find some other fool to give it to them. I'm resting here.

PIZARRO. Rest.

The text, then, is, on the whole, sound, though some effects are purely theatrical. At the entrance of the Inca, the dialogue does little to evoke the necessary burst of splendour and Shaffer relies heavily on visual resources to produce this climax. The humour of Pizarro's reluctance to copy Atahuallpa's energetic dance depends entirely on our having seen it performed, while the pathos of the moment where Pizarro collapses with his wound for the last time and Atahuallpa betrays the vital tenderness is rendered purely in terms of silent action. At another time, when Pizarro ties himself to Atahuallpa with a rope, Shaffer makes a stage property do the work of a metaphor; the rope is a concrete and telling way of showing that the two men stand or fall together.

However dependent *The Royal Hunt of the Sun* may be for some of its moments on fine acting and production, for the reader there are graphic stage directions which become an integral part of the play and successfully convey and sustain the mood.

A.W. England
1966

96

SCHEDULE OF MUSIC

LIST OF MUSIC IN SCORE

1. Recorded Organ Music (4 min. 45 sec.)
2. Opening of the Sun (35-40 sec.) – orchestra and chants
3. End of the Court scene (15-45 sec.) – orchestral
4. Atahuallpa's invitation to Pizarro – orchestral
5. The bird cries in the forest (up to 6 min.) – 4 tracks of recorded bird cries plus Indians on 'bird flutes' and guerros
6. Introduction to 'Toil Song' – orchestral
7. 'Toil Song' – Indian singing with small marracas and small drum
8. Villac Umu's Embassy: arrival (5 sec.)   orchestral
                         exit   (5 sec.)
9. Indian Chants of Praise – orchestra and chants
10. Offstage Spanish Te Deum – recorded Spanish chanting
11. Climbing of the Andes (up to 6 min.) – orchestral (2 flexatons)
12. Procession into Cajamarca (1 min.-1 min. 20 sec.) – orchestra, plus Indians playing bells, cymbals, 'thumb pianos', marracas (large)
13. The Massacre (1 min.-1 min. 30 sec.) – orchestra plus bells on Indians
14. 1st Indian Lament – chant
15. Atahuallpa's Command for Gold (35 sec.) – orchestral
16. Clothing of Atahuallpa and his meal – Indians hum and play crotales, 'musical plates' and 'thumb pianos'
17. 1st Gold Procession – orchestra plus Indian humming
18. 'Little Finch' song – Atahuallpa sings
19. 2nd Gold Procession – orchestra plus Indian humming
20. The Dice Scene – orchestra plus Indian menaces; Indians play bird flutes and guerros
21. The Garotting of Atahuallpa – orchestra
22. Indian Chants of Resurrection – orchestra and chants

INSTRUMENTATION OF SCORE
(Orchestra: four percussionists)

Indians play the following on stage
   2 drums (Indian 'tablas' or 2 pairs of bongos)
   2 suspended cymbals on 'Indian handles'
   2 pairs very large marracas
   1 pair very small marracas on long handles
   4 guerros

97

Schedule of Music

2 dozen bamboo 'bird flutes' (slide recorders) (these can be obtained from any shop specializing in folk craft from India)

2 'thumb pianos' (cigar box type sounding board with spring steel tongues which should be hit with light, hard sticks)

Orchestral instruments, divided between four percussion players

6 suspended cymbals
4 pairs of bongos
1 big drum
1 xylophone
1 **glockenspiel**
2 lion roar drums (string drums)
2 guerros
5 triangles
3 pairs crotales (small cymbals)
2 sets of sleigh bells
1 woodblock
4 slapsticks
1 large flexaton (musical saw; blade approximately 5 ft. 6 in. long)
1 small flexaton

The Massacre

All Indians have small bells sewn along their sleeves in the Massacre (and the Procession into Cajamarca). Insofar as their movements are rhythmed, and in time with the orchestral music, this helps to keep the centre of musical (as well as dramatic) attention on stage. There is a section in the orchestral score of the Massacre which is almost completely silent, to enhance this effect.

The Bird Cries in the Forest (1st Act)

The Dice Scene (*Ruminagui*) (2nd Act)

In both these scenes the Indians play loud interjections to word cues on both 'bird flutes' and guerros, as a counterpart either to the recording of bird cries, or the orchestral music, to bring closer the sense of threat and danger to the centre of dramatic attention.

Toil Song

98

Schedule of Music

As the Indians come on the stage they all hum this tune, accompanied by the two women, one woman playing small marracas (one marraca to each beat), the other beating the exact rhythm on a small drum (perhaps a 'tabla' wood drum). When work commences the two women sing the song twice, then all resume humming as the Spaniards speak until all workers are off stage.

LITTLE FINCH

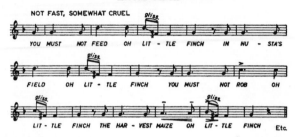

This should be sung very simply with no 'rubato'. Accentuation and dynamics must depend on the meaning of the words. The glissandi should be as the swooping of a bird of prey.

THE HUMMINGS

Atahuallpa's Dressing Scene and meal:

All Indians should hum this tune throughout the scene.

The Indians who help to dress Atahuallpa all have one pair of suspended crotales (ancient Chinese cymbals) hanging from each wrist (about 15 inches of string to each crotale). The Indians who bring on food and feed Atahuallpa have no crotales, but the gold plates should have many small bells hanging below the rims. The plates should also have double bottoms (the lower ones are drum skins). Dried peas or gravel should be inserted between the two bottoms, thus turning the plates into rattles. These plates should be 'played' as they are carried onstage and until Atahuallpa receives his first morsel of food. During Atahuallpa's meal, plates and crotales are silent, the humming continues accompanied by two 'thumb pianos' (pitch ad libitum, to the rhythm of the 'Toil song')

THE GOLD PROCESSIONS

Hum the TOIL SONG at a lower pitch, *slow*.

99

NOTES

*The notes in this edition are intended
to serve the needs of overseas students
as well as those of English-born users*

ACT 1

PAGE
1   *hidalgo:* a nobleman

    Save you all: a general salutation, probably shortened from 'God save you all'.

2   *Don Cristobal on the rules of Chivalry:* He'd made two expeditions.

3   *smith:* a person who shapes metal by hammering; probably a blacksmith.

    page: a youth training to become a knight by serving a person of higher rank as a servant or attendant.

    mercenary: a hired soldier in foreign service.

4   *Balboa:* see historical introduction.

    farrier: a person who shoes horses.

5   *cooper:* a person who makes or repairs casks and barrels.

6   *muster:* the assembly or roll-call of troops.

    lodestone: a piece of metal exhibiting magnetic properties, and by extension any object which has the power to draw men's desire to it.

7   *arquebus:* an early rifle-like firearm with matchlock fired from a portable rest near its muzzle; precursor of the musket.

8   *the austere polyphony of Spanish celebration:* Spanish church music was noted for its severe and grave simplicity. 'Polyphony' describes the combination of two or more independent melodies; it is music which appeals more to the intellect than to the emotions.

    Franciscan: religious order founded by St Francis of Assisi.

    the white cloaks of chivalry: worn by knights on solemn occasions to suggest purity of soul and body.

    the day of St John the Evangelist: 27 December 1530.

9   *Veedor:* inspector.

11 *Inca:* variously translated as 'King', 'Great Lord', 'Emperor', 'Monarch or King of Many Realms', applied correctly only to the divine head of state, but now used in the plural to describe the peoples ruled over by the King.

    Villac Umu: literally 'Guardian of Posterity', the title of the high priest.

    Challcuchima: one of Atahuallpa's generals.

12 *Chasqui:* The runners or couriers who in relays carried news and

Notes

short dispatches over the royal roads to Cuzco; they ran at fantastic speeds.

12 *huge sheep:* actually sheep were unknown to the Incas, as was the horse to which this is meant to refer.

Cuzco: the fabled capital of the Inca Empire, literally meaning 'The Fourfold' or 'navel', out from which ran the four great royal roads. See note to p. 20, below.

Capac: 'Chief' or 'Lord'.

Tumbez: on north coast where Pizarro first landed. See map.

13 *God's wounds:* a mild oath referring to Christ's wounds.

Huascar and *Inca Huayana:* see historical note.

Sapa Inca: 'Sapa' means 'the one' or 'only', thus the One true god-king.

Inca Capac: the 'Great' or 'Magnificent'.

15 *Cajamarca:* famous for its hot spring where Atahuallpa was resting after the conclusive battle in the Inca civil war. See map.

16 *Strozzi's most perfect model:* Filippo Strozzi, Florentine gunsmith who in 1530 improved the range and effectiveness of the arquebus.

17 *condor:* a very large vulture of the high Andes.

gobbets: hunks of raw meat.

18 *mimosa:* a tropical shrub or tree with prickly leaves and small flowers.

19 *I confess my people:* the Spaniards were surprised by the similarity of this rite to the Roman Catholic sacrament of Confession.

laws of the sun: life in an agricultural society was regulated by the seasons.

20 *harvests:* their principal crops were maize (corn) and potatoes, both indigenous to America.

herds: the llama and the alpaca.

tupu: probably about an acre.

four great roads: running from Cuzco to the end of the Inca Empire in Ecuador and Chile; they were twenty-four feet wide and equal the Roman roads in the daring of their engineering; whole armies could move over them quickly and they were the reason for the rapid expansion of the Inca Empire in such a short time as three centuries.

21 *Ware:* beware.

22 *Stay here:* the Spanish garrison at San Miguel.

24 *Viracochian Aticsi:* Great Viracocha.

Inti Cori: the 'Golden Sun', one of the names given to the Inca.

Caylla: Behold.

Huaccha Cuyak: Protector of orphans.

27 *eucalyptus trees:* large evergreens of the myrtle family.

29 *San Jago:* a famous war-cry of the 13th century.

Notes

PAGE

29 *Virgin of the Conception:* one of several titles given to Mary, mother of Christ, in the Roman Catholic Church.

31 *maggoty:* wormy.

32 *All Europe knows it:* not quite true; the Copernican and Galilean theory was known to learned scientists but not to the uneducated masses.

33 *Exsurge Domine:* Rise up, O Lord.
Deus meus eripe me de manu peccatoris: 'My God, deliver me from the hands of sinners.'
Many strong bulls have compassed me . . . dust of death. See Psalm 22:12-15.

35 *The Angel of the Apocalypse:* the angel which is supposed to prophesy the coming of the end of the world. See 'The Revelation of St John the Divine' at the end of the New Testament.

36 *marraccas:* a gourd shaped rattle used as a rhythm instrument.

37 *vassal:* a feudal servant who pledged homage and fealty to his lord.

38 *San Jago Y Cierra España:* an old medieval war-cry roughly translated as 'Santiago [San Jago] and at them'.

ACT 2

43 *I have a game here to amuse you:* a card game.
pyxes: vessels in which consecrated wafers (representing bread as the body of Christ) are kept pending their use at Mass. See note to p. 48, *biscuit.*
I would fill this room: variously reported as 17ft. x 22ft. x 9ft., 17ft. x 35ft. x 9ft.

45 *Quito:* now the capital of Ecuador.
Pachamacac: ancient holy temple to Pachamacac, Creator of the World, situated on the coast near present-day Lima.
Coricancha: the 'Palace of Gold' at Cuzco, one of the most splendid buildings in the kingdom with walls of gold and gold statuary in its garden.
Vilcanota: a holy oracle and shrine some sixty miles south west of Cuzco.
Colae: an Indian tribe of the southern highlands recently subdued by Atahuallpa.
Aymaraes: another tribe of the southern highlands traditional enemies of the early Incas.
Arequipa: due south of Cuzco, near the coast.
Chimu: the most important of the kingdoms of the coast with its capital at Chanclian; flourishing between 1200 and 1475, it was then brought into the Inca Empire.

Notes

46 *royal cloak:* of the finest vicuna wool.

vampire birds: the *curinquinque* bird, supposed by the Incas to be very rare.

his ears were hung again: large earrings to enlarge the lobe of the ear.

48 *a biscuit:* the wafer which represents the body of Christ and is taken at Communion in the Roman Catholic Mass.

51 *Anti-Christ:* believed by the early Christians to rise to great power immediately before the Second Coming of Christ. See II Thessalonians 2, I John 2:18.

54 *the dance of the aylu:* the *aylu* (or *ayllu*) was the social unit of the Incas similar in some ways to the Scottish clan.

55 *halberd:* a weapon consisting of a long pole with an axe or spear mounted on the end.

57 *Arabs:* the prized horses of the Mediterranean Arabs.

58 *chica* (or *chicha*): actually a mildly intoxicating maize beer.

63 *Sin Original:* the sin of Adam and Eve which, in Christian theology, all men are said to have inherited and which is removed by Baptism.

74 *your creed:* the Apostles' Creed of the Roman Catholic Church.

reins: the loins, then considered to be the centre of the affections.

76 *Ichu grass:* coarse mountain grass; the penitant spoke his sins into the grass, which was usually thrown into a nearby stream to be carried away as a symbol of the sins being absolved; the striking on the back with a stone was the usual penance endured by the penitent; the incantation referred to here went as follows: 'Hear me mountain peaks about, and plains, and condors which soar, and owls, for I wish to confess my sins.'

77 *Inti:* the Sun god.

EXERCISES

A *Character*

1. Pizarro's real inner conflict had begun long before the opening of the play; his dilemma concerning Atahuallpa serves only to bring his personal tragedy into sharper focus. Discuss.

2. Both Pizarro and Atahuallpa are seen ignoring repeated warnings at various parts of the play. What are they, and what are the results of their persistence in ignoring them?

3. In what different ways is Pizarro's treatment of Martin and de Soto similar to his attitude towards Atahuallpa? How does it differ from his attitude towards Valverde and Estete?

4. In what way is Pizarro's statement 'I do not know love' central to

the whole play. Is his feeling at the very end the same or different? Explain.

5. Despite their differences in age, what common bonds unite Atahuallpa and Pizarro.

6. In a personal sense what does Pizarro learn from Atahuallpa, and what does Atahuallpa gain from Pizarro?

7. What differences do you note in the character of Young Martin and Old Martin. What different dramatic purpose do each serve in the play?

8. As Pizarro loses his confidence and self-control, he loses control of his troops. Discuss.

9. The ending of the play cannot be considered truly tragic since Pizarro finds some kind of relief and inner peace. Discuss.

10. All the principal characters in the play – Pizarro, Atahuallpa, Young Martin and de Soto – end up by being rather different from their respective personalities as portrayed earlier on in the play. Each, in different ways, matures. Explain.

B *Themes*

11. How do the values of de Soto and Young Martin contrast with those of Valverde and Estete?

12. What comment does the play make about 'honour', 'hope', 'time' and 'trust'?

13. Discuss the apparent contradiction between the two following statements by de Soto and de Nizza respectively: (a) 'I have settled several lands. This is the first I've entered which shames our Spain.' (b) 'When I came here first I thought I had found Paradise. Now I know it is Hell. . . . What are your Inca's subjects? A population of eunuchs, living entirely without choice.'

14. In what sense are both the Christian and the Inca religion as seen in the play without love?

15. How does the author manage to unite both the personal conflict of Pizarro with the political and religious conflict of the play? Which seems more important, more absorbing?

16. Discuss the significance of the title. In what way can it be considered ironic?

17. In a broad sense, the play is really about the quest of a man for freedom from himself; personal salvation is seen therefore as the result of commitment to another human being. Discuss.

18. In what ways is Pizarro as much a victim as Atahuallpa?

19. There is a certain irony in the fact that while the Christians set out to conquer the heathen natives, Pizarro is himself converted by one. Discuss.

Exercises

C *Structure*

20. (*a*) What structural purpose does Old Martin's running commentary serve for the plot of the play? What other dramatic purpose is served by his wry observations? What effect do these ironic comments have on the involvement of the audience in the action and emotion of the play? (*b*) In what sense is de Soto a Horatio-like character?

21. Why is the episodic nature of the plot-development appropriate to the subject of the play? Why is the large number of scenes and the large cast of characters appropriate to the play?

22. Show what means Shaffer has employed to bridge time lapses and geographical shifts of scenic location. How does this resemble a Shakespearean play?

23. How does the essential conflict of Act II differ from that of Act I? How are they related? Explain how the plot of the two Acts of the play might be termed 'symmetrical'.

24. In any historical play such as *The Royal Hunt of the Sun* it is necessary to provide the audience with background information and character motivation which explains events and behaviour in the present. What means does Shaffer use to make this dramatic and interesting? Do you feel that he is wholly successful?

25. While Pizarro's real personal inner conflict is not revealed until Scene x in Act I, what hints are given in earlier scenes to suggest its quality?

26. By means of examples, show how Shaffer has relied heavily on irony of character, situation and language to create dramatic impact in this play.

D *Staging and Production*

27. How does Shaffer use the visual effect of the costumes to emphasize the political conflict between 'the active iron of Spain against the passive feathers of Peru'?

28. Choose two scenes which gain by the use of music and sound effects. Using a tape recorder, try to record one of these scenes and play it back to the class. Does your version conform to how the rest of the class imagined it?

29. To what use does Shaffer put the two acting areas in Act I? How does lighting help him to differentiate between them?

30. Discuss the effectiveness of the use of mime in the play. Do you think the 'voice over' commentary of Old Martin is necessary?

31. Consider how and why this play might readily lend itself to being adapted to the screen?

32. How necessary are the graphic stage directions to a private reader's enjoyment of the play?